EVALUATE
your brain fitness with a quick quiz

BALANCE
right and left brain functions

DEVELOP
your frontal lobe capability

IMPROVE
your synapse time

DAYDREAM
for fun and profit

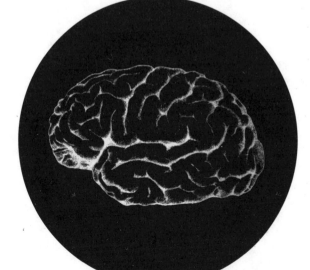

STRENGTHEN
your memory

The Brain Workout Book

THE BRAIN WORKOUT BOOK

Snowdon Parlette

M. Evans and Company, Inc.
New York

M. Evans and Company, Inc.

216 East 49th Street

New York, New York 10017

Library of Congress Cataloging-in-Publication Data

Parlette, Snowdon.

The brain workout book / Snowdon Parlette.

p. cm.

ISBN 0-87131-813-X

1. Thought and thinking. 2. Critical thinking. 3. Creative thinking.

4. Thought and thinking—Problems, exercises, etc.

I. Title.

BF441.P374   1997

153.4—dc21   96-51056

CIP

Design & typesetting by Annemarie Redmond

Manufactured in the United States of America

9 8 7 6 5 4 3

For Libby and Betty Anne

Steadfast and true

Many Thanks

CONTENTS

INTRODUCTION

So is this book supposed to make me smarter, turn me into a genius? Am I going to amaze my friends with incredible feats of mental gymnastics? And do I have to solve a bunch of killer brain teasers, memorize Latin verbs, slog through Einstein's theory of relativity until calculus equations start coming out my ears?

Relax, *The Brain Workout Book* is not about getting your Mensa club card nor is it a cram course for better SATs. These exercises are about making the brain work better, smoother, easier, happier.

Like a muscle workout, you can make the decision to tune your brain up, get the rust out, or you can take it into hyper-drive and build the body or, in this case, the mind beautiful. It's entirely up to you.

The Brain Workout Book exercises are designed to be useful, doable, and fun for everyone. It's not about getting smarter, it's about getting in shape.

All right, brass tacks. What is it about the brain? How come I need to exercise it? My brain seems to work fine, at least most of the time.

Start with this. Everything we are aware of, everything we know, everything we feel, everything we think happens inside a roughly three-pound, jellied mass we call the brain. This walnut-shaped organ is so delicate that without the bony mass of the skull to support it, it would simply gush away like so much melting Jell-O. And yet this amazing organ is what allows us our consciousness, our very sense of being. It is the seat of our existence, both worldly and inner worldly. In a nutshell, here is where we truly live. So, clearly, it's a good idea to keep this seemingly fragile and yet incredibly complex and powerful organ in top condition. After all, if it's well cared for, it's capable of operating non-stop for over one hundred years. If it's not well cared for, well, look around you.

Just consider for a moment all the things our brains are called upon to do for us. First of all, our brains allow us contact with that thing out there we call the world and with all the other people and creatures that appear to be inhabiting the realm just outside the lens of our eyes and just over the tip of our noses. It's a noisy place that sometimes smells and also causes sensations in those weird extremities that are somehow connected down there below our chins in that thing we call a body.

"A good mind possesses a kingdom."—Seneca

Amazingly, we can, simply by an act of will, make something down there, say a finger, wiggle! We can even set the whole mass in motion and walk across a room, a truly astounding feat, and all done by the power of the mind. In fact, by the age of four or five we become so used to making our body do our bidding that it ceases to amaze us. We begin to take for granted the extraordinary control we enjoy over our bodies and the physical world around us. It's no longer a big deal to reach out and touch someone. But if you can remember back to when you were three or four, you remember it was a very big deal indeed.

Which brings me to another remarkable brain feature, the ability to remember and to remember prodigiously. Forget volume, just think of all the different types of memories we are capable of storing in our brains. Memories of events, images, procedures, names, languages, perceptions like smell and taste, musical phrases, conclusions, stories, common sense, emotions, wisdom, jokes. In short, a whole lot of different things that ultimately shape us and make us what we are.

We remember and we become the sum total of our memories. Take away our memories, which sadly does happen to some unlucky people, and we become a stranger to ourselves.

And yet as important as memory is to us, we take the ability to process memories pretty much for granted. Most of us don't even think about memory except when it momentarily fails us. With a modicum of exercise we can keep our memory systems operating in top form and avoid those embarrassing moments like when we suddenly can't remember the name of a person we are about to introduce.

"Bill Johnson, this is…my good buddy…we've worked together for years…wives are best friends…."

This is your brain's way of saying it's time to tune up the old memory system.

We all know people who are talented in some way, artistically, athletically, or perhaps logically. We all have "gifts" for doing certain things well and conversely we are all klutzes at something—in my case, many things. These mental attributes and qualities also define and shape us just as memory does.

But what most people don't realize is that even if you don't have a talent for something, you can still learn to do it and do it well. Conversely, a talent not exercised will fade away.

In this respect, brain exercise is just as important as muscle exercise. Just like a muscle, if you don't exercise the brain, it will atrophy, at least the part you're not using.

"Use it or lose it" is as true of the mental faculties as it is of the physical ones.

"We are an intelligent species and the use of our intelligence quite properly gives us pleasure. In this respect, the brain is like a muscle. When it is in use, we feel very good. Understanding is joyous."—Carl Sagan

Fortunately, most of us do get plenty of stimulation in our daily routine, our jobs, our leisure activities, our relationships. The problem is our daily brain stimulation is often not very balanced. We may be exercising one part of our brain terrifically while letting other parts just sit there on the old couch and stare at reruns on television. This results in an imbalance which can actually effect our sense of well being. It can even make us physically ill.

The good news is that a brain, unlike a muscle, doesn't want to turn into Jell-O. A brain puts up a fight. It lets us know we are not giving it enough proper exercise.

We've all had that sense of irritability that comes from too much routine, too much drudgery. We've all said on occasion, "I need a change—I've got to shake things up—I'm bored—I need stimulation." Yes, that is your brain talking, and it's talking to you.

The question is what kind of stimulation and how much? This book provides exercises for all the major brain functions and at several different levels. You should be able to discover what's been missing for you, what part of your brain needs more exercise, or simply more stimulation.

You don't have to do all the exercises or do them in any kind of order. The idea of the exercises is to help you obtain a balance, a sense of well being. We've all experienced that warm glow in the body from a hard physical workout. *Brain Workout* exercises can provide that same glow for the brain and you won't even break a sweat.

(Incidentally, many of the *Brain Workout* exercises can be done simultaneously with a physical workout.)

The best idea is to try all of the different exercises and find the ones that work well for you. Who knows, you may even discover some native talents that you never realized you had, some long dormant skills that were just sitting there waiting to be developed. There's only one way to find out. So let's get started!

CHAPTER I

What's True; What's Not

A Few Basic Facts

There are many common myths and misconceptions about our brains and how they work. Let's start with our current fascination with computers. Some scientists think that computers will one day be just as smart as we are and even "think" as we do.

"Is my brain just a real smart computer?"

The answer is a definite no. Computers operate in a slavishly logical fashion and are unable to do what we call "reason." That is to say, they can't really think in the human sense of the word.

Fact: The Pentium processor, the current brain of the common desktop computer, is composed of about five million transistors. The human brain has more synaptic connections (similar to transistors) than the number of known stars in the Universe.

The Intel company has been making computer processors for about twenty years. The current model of the human brain has been in production for at least two hundred thousand years.

Computers do computations in an orderly step-by-step process in which no deviation from the "program" is allowed. Human brains act more like a large committee coming to a consensus after having considered all the relevant information and taking input from many different sources. We call this method of processing information a neural network.

The advantages are that we don't need every "committee member" to contribute equally all of the time. Some may be absent from a particular decision and yet the committee continues to function.

Still, the best committees are the ones where every member pulls his or her own weight. The exercises in this book are designed to stretch out and strengthen the various parts of our neural network just as if our brain were composed of a group of muscles.

Our brain power, like our muscle power, is derived from the sum total of all the units and, just like our body, certain parts of our brains are underutilized or out of shape. We can be mental couch potatoes just as easily as physical ones. This book is designed to help us burn some synaptic calories and in the process feel more alive and successful.

Since we're on the subject of how our brains work, what about all this talk of right brain and left brain? The right brain being our supposedly creative and emotional side and our left brain being our supposedly logical and coldly rational side.

"Do I really have two brains?"

A qualified yes. You do have two distinct hemispheres which are specialized for different types of information processing. These two major systems can more or less "think" by themselves, for awhile at least, and sometimes even hold opposite opinions. (Ever feel conflicted?)

"Okay, so who's in charge, right or left?"

The key thing to remember is that the two halves are connected. They exchange information and work together, in concert, to make one whole, we hope, well-rounded human being. Neither "half" dominates and both are absolutely essential to real-world problem solving.

"Yeah, well, I know some people that are definitely left-brain oriented."

People often think they have no talent for the artistic. Others think that their logical powers are deficient. This simply isn't true. They are just not utilizing the full potential of their brains.

The parts of our brain we use the least naturally aren't going to be very well developed. But that doesn't mean that the ability wasn't there to begin with.

Okay now, I'm not saying you are secretly Picasso or Einstein, but you aren't completely without talent, either. All of us have the same basic brain (with a just a few trillion trillion or so wiring variations).

That's why we can all appreciate things we ourselves can't do, such as hit a major league curve ball or write a moving line of music or come up with a clever way to build a mousetrap. We can certainly imagine doing those things and conversely, we can do a lot more than we imagine. All it takes is proper exercise.

"Is the old adage you can't do two things at once true?"

Yes and no. No, you cannot do two logical tasks at the same time because that would involve one specific neural network working on two problems at once. No can do.

However, some people can give the illusion of doing two logical tasks at the same time by training themselves to rapidly switch back and forth between two or even more tasks. (In much the same way a modern computer can multi-task by dividing up processor time.) Professional athletes do it for a living. But it is an illusion.

The human brain simply cannot think of two things to do at once without confusion and mis-coordination of information sent to the muscles. Witness the famous sports adage about the football player who is thinking about running for the touchdown before catching the ball and as a result flubs an easy catch and drops the ball.

Okay, so what about the yes answer?

We can indeed do two things at once as long as they don't involve the same brain hardware.

For example, we often listen to music while, say, balancing our checkbook; or view a work of art while discussing it. Both things are happening at once. We can take in emotions, music, visual and spatial concepts while operating our logic or language centers. In fact, we do it all the time.

It's so commonplace that we don't even realize we are doing it and we don't think of it as doing two things at once. But as we shall see in the left–right exercises to come, it is this dual functioning, this two things at once, that is the very basis of what we call creativity.

"What does it mean to be intelligent?"

There are strong myths as well as confusion when it comes to the subject of intelligence. Most people believe that intelligence can be tested and quantified. The test of choice is known as the IQ test. It is supposedly designed to measure your native or inborn intelligence. Your score, once established, is regarded as unchangeable throughout your entire life no matter what you do. But is this the whole story? Nowadays, researchers are not so sure.

"Isn't it true that some people are just born smart and the rest of us are stuck being plain old average?"

Not necessarily. You certainly can inherit skills and personality traits that last your entire life, but intelligence is a complex concept incorporating social beliefs and dogmas. For example, we base the IQ test on our own Western cultural values and on what we think of as common sense.

The trouble is, these values change from society to society and even from individual to individual within a society. For example, what is intelligent to an engineer or a scientist might seem like nonsense to a composer or a philosopher and vise versa. The rating of intelligence therefore is subjective. No test yet devised can accurately predict what a given brain is capable of doing across all the fields of human endeavor. Even a one-on-one comparison is usually meaningless.

Suppose we ask the question who was more intelligent, Michelangelo or Newton? The answer we get could depend on whether we ask a scientist or an artist. Of course, a really intelligent person understands that comparison between the two is impossible.

Personally, I like to think of intelligence as an individual measure of how we employ the brain power and the talents we have been given. In other words, intelligent people make the most of what they have. They often seem much smarter than they might test out to be. Many of the most successful people in all fields do not think of themselves as any smarter than you. They just use what they have to the fullest and, by the way, so can you.

Which brings us to a few quickly disposed of myths.

"Does brain power have to do with brain size?"

Nope. Smart people have all different size brains.

There is absolutely no correlation between brain or head size and intelligence or talent or anything mental.

"Do identical twins have identical brains?"

No. Because the brain continues to form throughout childhood and some researchers think throughout life, two brains that started out the same would quickly diverge. No two brains that ever existed since the dawn of time are the same and no two will ever be. We may look alike, but brain-wise we are all truly unique. There will never be another Shakespeare or, more comfortingly, another Hitler.

"Do mental powers decline with age?"

Not unless you are unfortunate enough to contract Alzheimer's or some other mentally debilitating disease. At one time researchers believed that brain cells slowly died off as we aged, leaving us old and inevitably senile. But it is now recognized that brain cells do not normally die off. The brain, it appears, can retain its full powers throughout life.

We can of course elect to kill lots of brain cells on our own by taking drugs, legal and illegal, and by poor nutrition. However, if we live a healthy, mentally active life, our brain should last at least as long as our body.

And as for teaching an old dog new tricks, current research shows that the human brain remains capable of learning new things well into the nineties and on a par with much younger brains.

And neither does memory necessarily fade with age. It's just that as you get older, you have more to remember and naturally more to forget.

By the way, forgetting is almost as important as remembering. We do it all the time. It's a way of cleaning house, getting rid of mental clutter. After all, we don't need to remember the vast majority of what we take in every day. Besides, there are some things we would all dearly love to forget. The good news is that if we keep our brains active and continually learning new things, we just might.

"Do video games have any value as brain exercise?"

Actually, yes. Video games improve hand-eye coordination, a definite brain function. They can also improve spatial visualization abilities, anticipation and reaction skills, rapid decision making, pattern recognition, and to some degree, short-term memory.

The problem here is a tendency to over-exercise, sometimes to the point of addiction. Video games can offer tremendous stimulation, particularly to the younger, developing mind. But unless you plan to be a fighter pilot or are involved in a field in which these skills need to hyper-develop, you want to be careful not to overuse selected areas of the brain while underusing some other equally important areas, such as those dealing with social interactions, imagination, and language, to name a few.

The catch word here is judicious. If you enjoy video games, by all means play them. But limit the time spent daily or weekly and balance it out with other exercises.

Also, consider interactive games with real live people. And I don't mean two-person video games. For an interesting change, try something low-tech like a card game, a board game, or a mind game like "Dictionary." (If you don't know about mind games, ask somebody born before 1955 for a complete list.)

These kinds of interactive games will pit you against much faster and craftier opponents than a mere computer. You'll develop many of the same brain areas to a much higher level.

As an added bonus, you'll also be exercising social and communication skills at the same time.

"What about television?
Does it really turn my brain into cookie dough?"

Well, maybe not cookie dough, but something close. Okay, television is really not such a bad thing. It actually can be mental exercise and, no, I don't mean you have to watch "educational programs" (although they certainly don't hurt).

In the Lazy Man's section there are exercises you can do while watching your favorite episode of "Seinfeld." No kidding.

However, the normal way of watching television falls under the heading of mental relaxation rather than mental exercise. But this is also an important brain function.

Television watching can be a useful way to cool down or turn it off altogether after a hard day. Muscles need rest periods and so does the brain.

The good news is that the majority of programming today most definitely falls into the category of brain resting. So when you need to, rest away. Again, as with video games, don't overdo it.

"Can drugs make me smarter?"

The mechanics of brain operation, as far as we know, is an electrochemical process. This obviously means that chemicals or drugs can have an effect on how the brain operates. We are still learning about how and what these effects are, but in general they have to do more with mood and perception than with actual performance.

It appears that psychoactive drugs like Prozac, Lithium, and others, properly administered, can be genuinely helpful to those unfortunate brains that have severe emotional problems. But can drugs make a normal brain perform better? Well, they might make you think you are performing better or, like caffeine, make you feel sharper, more alert, but these are really just mood changes and not performance enhancements.

Sure, I feel much more alert and ready to go after a cup of coffee, but if coffee is not available, I still manage to get going. And, in terms of stimulation, an exciting experience or event will get my synapses firing far more rapidly than a cup of Moca-Java at the local Starbucks.

As for other common stimulants like nicotine and alcohol or the illegal street drugs, the question becomes, "Are the perceived benefits worth the very real danger of damage those drugs can do to our bodies as well as our brains?"

And, since we can experience most if not all of the feelings produced in this artificial fashion by safer and more conventional means—that is by living life with our brains awake and alive—why seek a chemical solution?

All drugs can basically do for you is artificially increase your state of alertness or, conversely, dull it. Despite the claims of charlatans, drugs can't give you a super-charged memory or suddenly turn you into a math whiz.

My advice is, if you want to alter your mood for the better, do something different, something stimulating, like one of the exercises in this book. And if you're having serious problems with your moods, such as constant depression, then by all means, seek medical help. It is available. It does work.

As for really getting smarter, just exercise your brain, that's all it takes.

CHAPTER 2

EVALUATING YOUR BRAIN FITNESS

This section is designed for those who want to discover exactly what kind of shape their brain is in and set up a tailored exercise regime to improve it.

It is not necessary to go through this process if you already have an idea of the areas you would like to work on, or if you have the type of brain that prefers to explore and poke around on it's own. Just like down at the old exercise gym, not everybody likes to work out the same way. We try to accommodate all comers.

For convenience, the following chapters will begin with an explanation of what the particular exercises contained within them are designed to do. This should give you plenty of guidance if you just want to browse first before diving in.

What are we trying to do here?

A fit brain is reflected in a sense of general well-being, and in an eager willingness to experience fresh ideas and explorations. A fit brain welcomes new interactions, new challenges, new experiences. A fit brain quite simply enables us to enjoy life more completely and a fit brain lets us realize the full potential of our own particular gifts. Remember, we celebrate our mental uniqueness by utilizing our talents and our special abilities, not by keeping them dormant. Don't let them sit there like a bunch of flabby muscles.

Okay, the first task is evaluation. We need to know what kind of shape our brain is in, and which kinds of exercises might be most useful for our particular brain. Then it will be on to waking up those lazy, underused synapses and forgotten nodes. Time to do a little neural net conditioning!

Start by asking your brain the following questions. (Don't worry, even flabby brains can get though this.)

1. *How often do you describe an experience as exciting?*

    A Almost never   B Once in a while

    C Often   D Most of the time

2. *How often do you say to yourself "I'm bored"?*

    A Almost never   B Once in a while

    C Often   D Most of the time

3. *How often do you purposely do something different, something outside your daily routine?*

    A Almost never   B Once in a while

    C Often   D Most of the time

4. *Do you fully engage yourself mentally in whatever you are doing?*

    A Almost never   B Once in a while

    C Often   D Most of the time

5. *Do you fear making mistakes or errors of judgment?*

    A Almost never   B Once in a while

    C Often   D Most of the time

6. *When you meet someone new, either at work or socially, are you concerned about appearing stupid, or foolish, or ignorant?*

A Almost never   B Once in a while

C Often   D Most of the time

7. *Does the idea of a mental challenge such as being given more responsibility at work make you uncomfortable?*

A Almost never   B Once in a while

C Often   D Most of the time

8. *Do you avoid tasks that require aesthetic judgment or artistic skill?*

A Almost never   B Once in a while

C Often   D Most of the time

9. *Do logical tasks like mathematics, puzzles, or problem-solving make you cringe?*

A Almost never   B Once in a while

C Often   D Most of the time

10. *Do you have trouble making up your mind?*

A Almost never   B Once in a while

C Often   D Most of the time

11. *Do you have difficulty remembering information or events?*

A Almost never   B Once in a while

C Often   D Most of the time

12. *Do you enjoy playing games with other people?*

A Almost never B Once in a while

C Often D Most of the time

13. *Do you have trouble visualizing something that is being described to you, such as an object, a behavior, or perhaps an event?*

A Almost never B Once in a while

C Often D Most of the time

14. *Do hand-eye coordination tasks make you feel like a klutz?*

A Almost never B Once in a while

C Often D Most of the time

15. *Do you have trouble with organization either at work or in your personal life?*

A Almost never B Once in a while

C Often D Most of the time

16. *Do you actively plan and initiate what happens in your life?*

A Almost never B Once in a while

C Often D Most of the time

The purpose of these questions is primarily evaluation, so I will discuss the questions in some detail and make recommendations for a program tailored to your particular needs.

But for the benefit of those over-achievers among you who feel you must be rated, here is a scoring system that will give you an idea of what kind of shape "the little gray cells" are in (to quote that fictional master of mental aerobics, Hercule Poirot).

For questions 2,5,6,7,8,9,10,11,13,14, and 15, an A answer is worth four points, a B answer three points, a C answer two points and a D answer one point.

For questions 1,3,4,12, and 16 (in other words, all the rest) give yourself one point for an A answer, two points for a B answer, three points for a C answer, and four points for a D answer.

Now for the tricky part, add it all up. Come on, I promise this is the only required math in the whole book.

Okay, here's the short answer.

If you scored 60–64, give this book to a needy friend, you're in great shape. In fact, I bet people line up just to feel your massive frontal lobes.

45–59: Very good, you've reason to be proud of that little bundle of nerve fibers you got up there, but you can still benefit from some tune-ups in specific areas.

33–44: Like most of us, you've been spending much too much time on the couch. You need to get in the game. It's time to start doing some stretches, get that brain aerobicized, and make those sorry synapses start popping! You need to feel some burn. Fortunately, I've got a program for you.

20–32: Very bad shape. In fact, I'm assuming you've just woken up after being in a coma for at least seven years because the lowest you can score is a fifteen (which would mean you were still in a coma). Go very slowly, but the good news is you've got nowhere to go but up.

Okay, now the step-by-step evaluation. Questions one and two are, of course, very general and designed to make you think about how you view your mental state overall.

1. Whereas few people outside of stunt doubles and maybe major rock stars can truthfully answer that most of their daily experiences are exciting, it is a question of perception.

However, if your brain is working up to it's potential then most of what you do feels exciting to you simply because you are reveling in using that wonderful organ.

I can liken it to a person who does regular body exercise and derives a strong high from it. Since you employ or should employ your brain with even greater frequency, you should experience most of life as at least stimulating, if not downright exciting. If you're not, then it's time to shake things up. You need to have your interest seriously piqued, so do any and all of the exercises that your poor, deprived synapses find stimulating.

"It is not enough to have a good mind; the main thing is to use it."—Descartes

2. Conversely, the second question should be an unequivocal A—Almost never.

If you are bored even as often as B—Once in awhile—then you need to find some more mental stimulation. You are probably sitting on a couple of major areas of brain function that you don't even realize are there.

You will benefit by trying some of the exercises that seem most foreign to you, most out of the ordinary, most unusual. You need to try some things that you are convinced you cannot do and surprise yourself.

Once you open up these new channels, you'll have to really work at being bored from now on.

3. Question three deals with how much "different" you allow into your life.

The brain thrives on new situations, new problems, new explorations. This is where you really see how strongly the brain differs from a mere computer.

Computers need very specific parameters. Our brains need only very general parameters and thrive on experiencing the unusual.

We need to constantly expand our horizons, expose our brain circuits to new challenges.

Now, of course, we don't have to explore the Amazon basin or trek across Tibet on a camel in order to shape up our brains, although that is one great way to do it, assuming your finances allow.

It is also possible, however to have "exotic" experiences closer to home and even to fit them into a tight schedule.

Quite a few of the exercises are designed to give the brain a solid dose of "Strange" without the danger of mosquito bites or traveler's diarrhea.

For those brains that find themselves in too much of a daily rut, check out the exercises in Chapter 3.

4. Now we are going to get into some specifics. If you have trouble engaging your mind or trouble concentrating, then you may need work on the frontal lobes where initiation, will, and most of what we call our "human desire" is located.

This area is what most strongly differentiates us from other creatures on planet earth. We're the only ones that got them, so let's make good use of them. All the other animals are very jealous.

Exercises that improve concentration and motivation can be found throughout this book.

You would also probably benefit from some social interaction exercises. Often engagement problems come from doubt, doubt about our ability to "read" the situation. Try some of the game exercises in Chapter 14.

You could be disregarding or downplaying what your emotional processors are telling you. In other words, a classic right–left brain conflict that leaves you paralyzed in certain situations. If this is the case, try some exercises from Chapter 6.

5. This is a biggie. Unfortunately, fearing mistakes is common in our society, but I'm going to let you in on a secret. The brain only learns by making mistakes. How can you know something's right if you don't know what's wrong?

"A life spent making mistakes is not only more honorable but more useful than a life spent doing nothing."—George Bernard Shaw

By making mistakes, our neural nets are able to reconfigure themselves in order to do better next time. The brain does literally rewire itself every time we make a mistake and that rewiring is what we call learning. It's how the brain works, by trial and error.

All right, so first you have to get over worrying about being wrong. You need to engage in exercises where you can safely be wrong.

If the problem is other people, so-called friends giving you a hard time about making mistakes, then get some new friends. To err is human. Believe it. Because without errors, your neural nets go nowhere.

6. Okay, here we have the problem of confidence. Do we lack confidence in our brain because we think it's deficient, or because we secretly know it's badly out of shape? Well, if you think you're deficient, you're probably wrong. It's almost always a case of underdevelopment, or under-utilization. Hey, maybe you're not a rocket scientist,

but Forrest Gump showed us that even a really low IQ brain isn't stupid and has nothing to apologize for. If you're worried about how other people see your brain, it's probably because you know you haven't been doing much with it. So start shaping up. You'll need to do a little discovery. Try some general, major area exercises such as Chapter 7 on Visualization. Do some memory work (Chapter 8). Imagination exercises (Chapter 9) and try some Right brain–Left brain double-team exercises to get some synaptic energy flowing (Chapter 6).

"Everyone is ignorant, only on different subjects."
—Eleanor Roosevelt

7. Okay, this is another frontal lobe area related somewhat to Question 5. If fear of failure is the problem, then also try Chapter 14. If, however, complexity and challenge make you uneasy, then you need to do some complex and challenging exercises to convince yourself that you can handle them. Try Chapter 5.

8. I know, you've got no artistic sensibility, right? Wrong, we all have artistic sensibility, like it or not. It's a major part of our brain's function. We use it all the time without even being aware of it. An awful lot of functionality is tied to this ability. For example, we wander around exploring a new space and we make choices to move based on what draws our esthetic sense. We chose food because we "like" how it smells and tastes and looks.

Even if other people don't share our so-called "taste," we have it. We like things and we don't like other things—purely based on how they look, smell, feel, sound, and taste. That is artistic sensibility.

Now I will agree that if you answered C or D to this question, you are definitely not tapping into these neural circuits any more often than absolutely necessary. You could benefit from several exercises. Try Chapter 4 and see if you don't surprise yourself.

9. Flip side of Eight. You think you're no good at puzzles, math, stuff that requires heavy logic and problem-solving. What you probably don't realize is that the logic and problem-solving neural circuits are used heavily by artists as well as scientist and engineers. Einstein believed that the mental work he did had much in common with what an artist does and he was right.

People think of logical or mathematical problem-solving as absolute because the end result is sometimes expressed in an absolute. In other words, it's right or wrong, no gray area. In fact, that's not really true. Most logical problems, like artistic ones, have more than one solution. That's what makes them creative. The difference is really procedural. Problem-solving involves analysis—which is what the left brain excels at. The way to take the sting out of analysis is to view it as simply an exercise. When we expect results, especially immediate results, we often break into a cold sweat. It isn't necessary to put that pressure on ourselves. We can simply exercise the logic circuits for fun and get very good "results" by just getting in shape. As to that fear you have of arriving at an incorrect answer, I'll let you in on a big secret. There aren't any.

10. The old right–left conflict rears it's ugly head. We all have experienced anxiety over making a fateful decision at some point in our lives. It usually comes when we are confronted by a difficult or important question such as, "should I change jobs or marry this person?"

But if you often have trouble making up your mind, then you probably are not experiencing very good information flow between the two brain hemispheres. If the two sides can't talk to each other freely, then how can they trust each other? All of a sudden a consensus is required, a decision must be made, and your brain feels confused, conflicted. Well, guess what, it probably is.

Just as in a relationship, the three most important things for a happy brain are Communication, Communication, and Communication.

You need to help your brain bridge the gap, actively encourage some dialogue up there. If you're feeling doubts, talk to yourself about them, find out what's going on. Sound like shrink-time? Well, that's pretty much what therapy is about, unclogging the pipeline.

That's why therapists talk about getting in touch with your feelings or trusting your feelings. What they are really saying is that the left brain, the logical part, isn't getting enough input from the emotion-decoding right side. Now, obviously, if the problem is severe or disabling, proper physiological therapy is warranted. However, most of us just need to do some exercise to get the circuits humming up there in the old Corpus Callosum. (That's the bridge or, if you like, the phone line between the two brain hemispheres.) The left–right brain exercises should do the trick if you will get your brain to do them.

11. Poor Memory? Probably because it's not getting enough exercise. Turn to Chapter 8 and start doing some exercise. What's in a memory? Only your whole life. And if you don't use it, you will lose it. Remember, keep it strong.

12. Interactive games serve many purposes for the brain. First, there is the obvious exercise of skill and

strategy. But also, there is the social interaction with other brains that brings in a myriad of circuits and very strongly exercises the left–right connection.

You may be called upon to exercise both judgment derived from the logical rules of the game and feelings (hunches) derived from the emotional signals given by the other players.

It is excellent brain exercise as long as you can freely participate. It's, in fact, one of the principal exercises we do which is why there are so many games, ranging from the very physical (like contact sports) to the almost purely mental (like chess).

Sadly, many people feel they cannot join in such exercise because they are afraid of failure (looking foolish in front of others) or they fear that they are too competitive, unable to accept defeat gracefully.

Both of these limitations can be overcome if you view game-playing as brain exercise. The goal when exercising is not to win, but to engage, to play.

Winning is only a very imperfect method to indicate progress in skill development. But, as we know, improvement comes with the doing whether or not you win the game. Therefore, there is no such thing as losing.

The trick to taking the fear out of it is to find games in which you can feel comfortable and competitive. Also, you need to find other participants of a like mind, that is, more concerned with enjoying the exercise and the community than with scoring points. A full discussion of game-playing as exercise in Chapter 14 explains how to change your attitude about games so that you can take advantage of this very engaging and very invigorating brain exercise.

13. Visualization skills have become more and more important in the complex world we live in. We are daily

forced to navigate new and complex architectural spaces. We are confronted with more product choices and more complex design possibilities. We need to visualize what's happening both in real time and for future possibilities. Architects, designers, engineers, builders, and artists have to do it for a living. So are there exercises to help. Some of the best are the ones used by the pros. See Chapter 7 for tips on how to put things in perspective.

14. Getting our bodies to do what our brain wants it to do is a problem we start wrestling with a few seconds after we leave the birth canal. Most of early childhood is spent learning to control our bodies.

Unfortunately, once the basic skills of walking and getting food into our mouths have been mastered, many of us found this a convenient time to head for the couch and begin a long career in front of a television screen. And even if our vice was something more socially presentable, such as reading all the time, we still neglected our hand–eye coordination training to the point that we now shy away from anything that requires rapid reflex response.

Although our mental life can be quite fulfilling even with no operational physical skills (witness the remarkable career of Stephen Hawkings), it does seem a shame to let perfectly good neural networks languish unnecessarily.

Even if you don't want to try anything complex, like a physical sport or, say, playing the piano, you should do some sort of skill exercise. In the skill memory section of Chapter 8 you will find a whole rash of suggestions. Too complex? Then try something simple and fun like the "Other hand day" exercise in Chapter 10.

15. Organization and planning are why you have those big frontal lobes that the other primates only dream about. These are circuits that simply must be exercised.

Many times, people feel they are poor planners or organizers because they are often stuck planning or organizing things that are not interesting or fun for them. The result is that since organization is regarded as drudge work, it's done poorly and laboriously and little is gained in the way of improved skill.

What your brain needs to discover is that planning and organization don't have to take a lot of time and don't have to be torture. If you can make it fun and interesting, then you can learn to do it well. One way to do this is to change the way you plan and organize. Try discovering a new way of planning, one that is organic to your brain. Start by observing how other people plan and organize. Ask them, if you can do so comfortably, to show you their methods, their techniques. If you do this enough, you will stumble on something that makes sense for you and you will suddenly have new inspiration, new energy. Ninety percent of problem-solving is how you initially approach the problem. So change the way your brain looks at things.

To aid your uninspired brain in finding new ways to look at problems, try some attitude-adjusting exercises. Also, the exercises on daydreaming will be very useful, believe it or not. Try them and see.

16. If you are not taking charge of your life, if you are just going with the flow, then your brain is probably on cruise control. For the sake of your neurons if nothing else, get out there and start exercising. Shake things up. Start with the daydreaming exercises. Initiation begins with inspiration. Then try some exploration exercises such as the ones in Chapter 3. Also do some group mind exercises, play some games. Contact with other minds leads to new ideas, new possibilities.

But whatever you do, get out there and get that mind stimulated. Exercise!

THE UNFAMILIAR: HOW TO MAKE A HABIT OF IT.

The major way we exercise our total brain is by experiential stimulation. Basically we do stuff, we go places, we see people, and we have some kind of experience.

Then we come home and mentally digest the information. Our brain will then sort through what happened, sleep on it, and sometime during the next few days make a decision about how much of it we need to remember.

The trouble is we all have a tendency to settle into routines. We go to the same places, see the same people, do the same things, over and over again. Our brains aren't exactly overtaxed with new experiential information.

"Experience is not what happens to a man,
it is what a man does with what happens to him."
—Aldous Huxley

Some of us no longer even remember the trip to and from work because it is so ingrained in us that it requires next to no conscious thought. Our brains are simply running on automatic, following well-worn routines that require very little energy, a virtual trance-like state. Ever hear the expression, I could do that in my sleep? Well, guess what, in this state your brain practically is asleep. Not that I'm knocking sleep, it's a good and valuable thing, but it is not exercise.

For exercise our brain wants stimulation, fresh stimulation, new stimulation. Our brain needs to experience the unfamiliar, go where it has not gone before.

It is by virtue of new and unfamiliar experiences that the brain constructs and expands its neural pathways and thus increases its capability. Every time we experience something new, the brain must do some serious work. It must take in, sort, and store a lot of brand-new information.

This causes a ripple effect as the brain is forced to reevaluate what it already knows and make modifications to its decision-making circuits. New possibilities are imagined, exciting the brain's creative circuits into action, and often leading to a wonderful feeling of expansive exultation.

"Make it a point to do something every day that you don't want to do. This is the golden rule for acquiring the habit of doing your duty without pain."—Mark Twain

Remember, a stimulated brain makes us feel more alive, more positive, more confident in our mental abilities. Putting it in more basic terms, it's a legal and healthy high.

Now, when I speak of new and unfamiliar experience, I mean of course good experiences, positive experiences, not overwhelming ones that induce a sense of fear or danger.

When the brain is forced into a defensive mode, it falls back on some of it's most primitive and instinctive systems. These systems are automatic and when functioning properly kick in without any willful action.

It is not the purpose of this book to exercise these brain circuits. They are emergency overrides, safety nets, and as such should be modified only with extreme caution.

If you have trouble with these circuits, if you are overly fearful or experience serious phobias, then, please, seek competent medical help.

Okay, so how do we shake things up, get some "strange" going?

Well, we already know that exotic trips to foreign lands bring us face-to-face with the new and unfamiliar, as does changing jobs or professions, or even just plain meeting an interesting new person. But what can we do on a daily basis to stave off the mundane, the creepy-crawly familiar bug?

We're going to list a few different exercises to help us get a healthy dose of unfamiliar into our daily lives. It doesn't take that much. In fact, it can be as simple as putting on a turn signal.

Before we start, one basic rule holds throughout the book. If an exercise doesn't grab your particular brain then don't force yourself beyond an initial, "what the hell, I'll give it a try."

If it doesn't work for you, move on to an exercise that is more suited to your brain's interest circuits.

Remember, just like physical exercise, if it's tedious, you won't do it. It has to be not only challenging, but in some way fun.

Exercises

EXERCISE

1

Beginner

Homeward Bound

To get out of the rut, all you have to do is change your route.

Okay, this sounds simple and it is, but the effects can be stronger than you think. At least once a week, take a completely different route home from work. (You can do this on the way to work as well, but most people are pressed in the morning and can't get the full benefit.)

Take a route that involves as many new streets as possible. In fact, go out of your way if possible.

En route, pay close attention to everything you see, businesses along the way, landmarks, buildings, new construction.

Note what goes on in the places you pass. If you like making a game of it, pretend you have just moved to a completely new town and need to learn where stuff is. If possible, go down streets you have never gone down before, or ones that you have rarely been on.

Intermediate

Expand this to include stopping somewhere along the way, somewhere different, a store or building. Go in and look around; if it's a store, browse.

Examine the architecture if it's a public building or explore the space if it's a park. (Churches are a good place to stop as they generally encourage visitors.)

If you see someone friendly, even a sales clerk, ask a question and engage in a short conversation.

Stay as long as you like. Leave as soon as you are ready. Not everywhere you stop will turn out to be interesting to you, but eventually some place will surprise you.

Return in your leisure time to a store, a business, or an organization that interested you. Learn more about it. Ask questions, find reading material.

Advanced

Think about what it might be like to work in that location or for that organization. Imagine being a part of it and think about how different your life would be there.

Imagine owning the business, or running the organization.

As you go to sleep that night, think about it and see if you can dream about it.

Just Looking

2

Beginner

▶ Go into a store that you normally never would go into, one that sells things you believe you have no need for.

Browse and examine as many new or different things as you can. If possible, pick things up and feel them. If you don't know what something is used for and are comfortable, ask a salesperson what it does. It's okay to tell them you are just browsing, or say you are getting ideas for a project.

Good stores for finding unfamiliar stuff are hardware and tool stores, professional stores like restaurant or office supplies, paint or decorator supplies, art supplies, medical-supply stores, photography stores, toy or hobby stores (if you're an adult), cloth and sewing supplies, garden centers, and nurseries.

You get the idea, just something that to you is unusual and different. Try to imagine using the products you discover.

Intermediate

▶ Investigate an organization or club with which you are unfamiliar. This can be a charity organization, the local chamber of commerce, or a historical society.

A really good one is to simply visit or attend a service at a church or synagogue or mosque that is not your faith. Even if you happen not to be religious, this is an interesting experience.

Remember, you don't have to join the organization; you are just going on an expedition. You are an explorer. You are seeking information.

Go with an open mind, ask questions and find out something about how it works, or what they believe, or what their purpose is. Smile a lot.

Go home and think about what you learned, review the experience in your mind, and decide how you feel about it. Feel perfectly free to dismiss it entirely if you so choose, but experience it. Make your brain do some work.

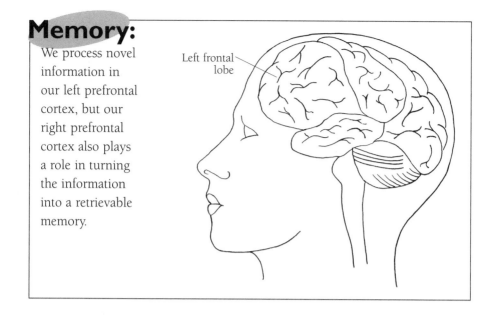

Memory:

We process novel information in our left prefrontal cortex, but our right prefrontal cortex also plays a role in turning the information into a retrievable memory.

Left frontal lobe

Advanced

Plan a foray into the unknown. Work out a day trip (longer if you like or can). Pick something of interest to see, something perhaps you've been thinking about or have always wanted to do. Now is the time to do it. Plan it and do it. Take someone along if you want, but concentrate on the experience more than the companion. This can be as simple as an extended walk in the country. But you must plan a route, expect to visit certain sites, and explore as much as possible. The more unfamiliar the ground, the better.

EXERCISE

3

The Re-Familiar

Wander about your house, apartment, backyard, garage, or attic and look specifically for things you have forgotten about or didn't know were there. Examine whatever you find carefully. If it's an object, recall how you got it. Re-familiarize yourself with it. Why was it forgotten? Why you don't use it? Use it if possible. If it's a book, read at least two pages.

4

A Simple Bookstore Exercise
(for the less mobile)

Go to your local bookstore (or library) and find the travel section. Browse. Find some picture books showing views of the various destinations. You know, seashores, mountains, pretty little towns, that kind of stuff.

Find a location that you like, one that speaks to you, calls you.

Now, find a map and figure out how you would get there from where you are. Plan in your mind how you would go, car, plane, etc. Think about what you might need to take with you.

Think about how long you want to be there.

Later on, while sitting quietly, remember the picture again. Try to see it clearly. Imagine that you actually have been there and that you would really like to go back. Think about what it smelled like there, how the wind was blowing, how sun felt on your face.

Imagine you are about to take a friend there. Describe to them what they are going to experience.

5

For The Very Advanced

Try something completely new. Explore the adult education courses available in your area. Get a brochure, yes, do it. Read through it carefully and thoughtfully; pick something that interests you. One hopes something you know little or nothing about except that it has always seemed interesting. Now go on down and enroll.

Remember, if it turns out to be less interesting than you thought, you can always drop it.

Also, remember you are not there to get a grade or be judged in any way. You are there for pure stimulation. If they don't deliver, in your opinion, then ask for your money back and look for something else, something different.

> *"If you haven't found something strange during the day, it hasn't been much of a day."*—John Wheeler

A personal note on this one. My father, who spent his life as a businessman, wearing a suit every day, at age sixty went down to the local community college and enrolled in class on brick laying. He said he had always wanted to know how to do it. Well, now he knows and he had a great time finding out.

Is he out there laying bricks you ask? Hell no, he hasn't touched a brick or mortar since the class ended. He just wanted some "strange" and he got it.

All right, I think you're getting the idea here. These are general exercises on the order of saying, "Hey, get your butt off the couch and go out and do some exercise, anything, just exercise!"

The rest of the exercises in this book will be aimed at improving specific brain functions.

CHAPTER 4

THE ARTISTIC YOU—WAKING UP THOSE RIGHT-BRAIN LOBES!

Two Halves Make A Whole

Yes, we do have a dual nature, a split personality if you will. This is because our upper brain is physically divided into two hemispheres which we sometimes refer to as the "Right" and "Left" brain.

But even though the two halves of our brain are highly specialized and are even capable, to some degree, of holding independent thought, it's important to remember that they form an inseparable unity.

The two halves form one whole brain.

Still, there are some significant differences between the left and the right hemispheres that need to be understood if we want to fully exercise our brain's capabilities.

To start with, each hemisphere actually sees the world differently. Or to be more precise, each half structures reality differently.

Basically the right half of our brain perceives the world as a whole and is

The Left Side

The left half of our brain is designed to break things down into component parts for analysis and sequencing. Some of its known specific duties include:

- All activities involving detailed logical analysis, such as working out an algorithm or following a story line.
- Sequential processing, such as the ability to follow a set of logical instructions.
- The interpretation of language and the generation of speech.
- The ability to read and write.
- The ability to sight-read music.
- The ability to count and to do mathematics.
- Symbol recognition.

quickly able to grasp totality. This allows us to recognize visual and auditory patterns and to process emotional feelings.

"Imagination is more important than knowledge."
—Albert Einstein

The left half of our brain breaks information down into component parts for analysis and sequencing. This allows us to follow a flow and to make logical sense out of what's happening.

Both views are necessary in order to have a full and complete understanding of what's going on out there in that place we call the real world.

In a healthy, well-exercised brain, these two "Realities" are seamlessly combined, giving us the ability to handle just about any situation that comes down the pike.

The Right Side

The right half of our brain is designed to perceive the world as a whole and to be able to grasp totality quickly. Some of its known specific duties include:

- The recognition of spatial relationships, which, among other things, gives us the ability to read maps, do jigsaw puzzles, and copy designs.
- Non-verbal sound interpretation, such as the ability to distinguish and remember musical tones, the appreciation of complex musical sounds, and the recognition of natural sounds.
- The recognition of faces.
- The generation and perception of emotions.

- The ability to visualize in three dimensions and the management of depth perception.
- Creating the experience of dreams.
- Creating the sense of body image and the ability to orient one's position.
- The ability to appreciate the visual arts.
- The management of long-term memory of events.

So even though you may think of yourself as a "Left Brainer" or a "Right Brainer", the truth is you are both.

You can't be "creative" without some sequential processing and you can't be "logical" without the ability to grasp the overall idea.

Problem-solving, whether it be artistic, scientific, or just plain practical, always involves both sides of the brain.

And both sides need exercise. In this chapter, we'll start with the right.

We're going to get those "artistic" neurons firing properly and have some fun in the process!

Exercising Those Right-Brain Specialties

Now when we isolate out the right side of our brain for these exercises, the left brain doesn't just get to take a nap. On the contrary, the left side is going to be getting a pretty good workout as well.

What we are actually going to be doing here is letting the right side of our brain call the shots. Both sides are working, but the right side is, so to speak, "in charge."

That means our left brain will be basically putting it's resources at the disposal of our right brain and acting like an executive assistant.

Now if your left brain is used to being in charge all of the time, that is to say, you are a "logical" type, you may have to work a little to get your left brain to let go and "trust" your right brain to run the whole show for a change.

Try to reassure your left brain that it will have plenty to do and that artistic endeavors really do require lots of sequential and logical processing. (Fun stuff for a left brain!)

And if nothing else works, try bribery. Tell it there'll be a crossword puzzle later on if it will just play ball for a little while.

Draw Pardner!

Put away your six guns and get out a Number Two pencil. Yes, we're going to do some drawing!

What do you mean you don't think you can do it?

If you're reading this, then I presume you are literate, which means besides reading, you can also write. And what is writing?

That's correct, all those funny little symbols you've been putting down on paper since you were a schoolkid are little-bitty drawings. You were always an artist and just never knew it!

Okay, so since you already have a basic idea of how to handle a pencil and a piece of paper, all we have to do now is make a minor change in what you do with these familiar implements.

Beginner

This one is simple and fun.

Take a sheet of paper larger than your hand. Place your hand, palm down, on the paper with your fingers spread out.

Now, hold the pencil upright and carefully trace the outline of your hand and as much of your wrist as the paper allows.

Remove your hand from the paper and place it nearby where you can see it clearly.

Now draw in all the details. Draw your fingernails and all those curvy lines around your finger joints and knuckles. Draw any skin markings, freckles, moles, birthmarks, tattoos, anything and everything that you see on the back of your hand. If you're wearing a ring, draw it in. If you have a watch on, draw that, too.

If you want some extra points, lightly sketch in the vein and tendon patterns. You could even go for a little shading if you like.

When you are done, do the other hand, yes, you'll have to initially trace out the hand with the one you aren't used to using! No fair getting someone else to do it for you!

Do this exercise twice a week for six weeks. You can simply repeat it, making the same drawing again and again or—if you want to add some variation and fun—try these suggestions.

Turn your hand over, do the palm side.

Next, don't make an initial tracing—just start drawing freehand!

Try holding your hand in different positions. You can even decorate your hand or put a glove on it and draw that!

You'll find that your hand is a very accommodating and patient model. Probably the best one you'll ever meet.

Intermediate

········► This is a limbering-up exercise that all artists are taught in Drawing 101. (Translation, it's really easy.)

It's not a whole lot different from plain old doodling. In fact, once you get it down, you can do this exercise while you are on the phone, while you're watching television, or any old time you want.

The difference is that, unlike your doodles, you may actually want to frame some of these exercise drawings.

Now, since you aren't a professional artist, you probably don't have folio-size sheets laying around. But, not to worry, ordinary eight-and-a-half-by-eleven typing or copy paper will work well enough. (Steal a few sheets from your office printer if you have to.)

You can, of course, use larger sheets of paper if you have them or want to buy them. It is true that the larger the paper the better. (Student artists use pads made of newsprint for this exercise because it is cheap and they are usually poor. You can get them at any art supply store.)

Now what we're going to do here is known in the trade as "gesture" drawings.

Sounds fancy, but actually they are easy to do and lots of fun besides. The idea behind gesture drawing is to get your pencil moving rapidly and freely around on the paper. It's a limbering-up exercise. Accuracy, you'll be happy to hear, is actually discouraged.

Gesture drawings usually end up looking like a pile of string, a kind of crazy wire model of whatever it is that you are drawing. That image should give you an idea of the effect you will be trying to achieve.

Okay, set up your paper on a tabletop, on the back of this book, or from wherever you decide you're going to launch your artistic career.

Now go into the kitchen and get yourself something to drink, a soda, a glass of water, okay, a beer if you want. Pour it into a glass and bring it back to the table.

No, don't drink it yet. Set it up about eighteen inches away where you can see it clearly. This is your very first subject!

Okay, presumably the glass has a round bottom and a round top which, as you are now viewing them, appear as ovals. We'll start with the bottom of the glass.

Place your pencil somewhere toward the bottom of the paper, not too close to the edge. Now get your whole hand moving in a big, sweeping, circular motion and start drawing ovals, one on top of the other.

You repeat the same oval in the same spot over and over again without stopping. Go around five, ten, fifteen, twenty times, it doesn't matter.

The idea is to just free up your hand and keep it moving smoothly. Don't hesitate and don't stop. Keep that pencil moving at all times.

Keep coming around that corner and making that oval again and again. Meanwhile, look at the glass and compare. With each revolution try to make your latest oval a little bit more like what you see.

Now at some point, basically whenever you feel like it, just suddenly start spiraling your pencil upward on the paper toward the top. You can move up slowly or fast, but keep on ovaling (it's now a spiral) until you think you've reached the top rim of your glass.

Okay, now stop moving up, but keep on ovaling. You're doing the same thing, going round and round. Try not to think, try to just keep your pencil moving.

At some point, move your ovaling down a little bit to where you think the line of the liquid is and make some more ovals there. (After all, the glass isn't empty, at least not yet.)

Now just keep going around with your pencil and move down again so that the part with the liquid in it has more spirals and is therefore darker. If it's really dark, like cola, then lots more spirals. If it's water, then fewer.

Okay, now at some point pretty soon here, your paper is probably going to become just about completely covered with pencil lead. (Don't worry, it's suppose to look that way.) Stop, turn the paper over (or get a fresh sheet if you prefer) and start again.

Now that you have an idea of what you are trying to do, see if you can capture the entire form of the glass a little quicker, with a few less strokes.

Remember, you still have to keep that pencil moving and you are still going to have lines all over the place. But don't worry about it.

It is the form of the glass that you are going to capture, not the exact shape. And don't worry about all the extraneous lines all over the place. They actually add interest. Just

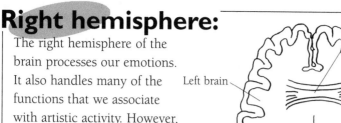

Right hemisphere:

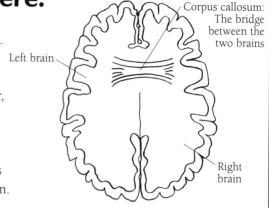

The right hemisphere of the brain processes our emotions. It also handles many of the functions that we associate with artistic activity. However, since the right hemisphere is unable to process language, right brain activity often registers in our consciousness as just a feeling or an intuition.

Left brain

Corpus callosum: The bridge between the two brains

Right brain

concentrate on trying to rough in the form of the glass with a constantly moving pencil.

By the way, you can vary the circular motion as much as you like—even make figure eights. Just remember you are really trying to draw a "wire form" in the shape of a glass or, if you prefer, a glass full of string.

Okay, so now keep on going. Make at least a dozen drawings all in the same manner.

Do no more than three drawings of the same object in the same position. You must either pick something else to draw or move to a new location so that your view is changed and the object looks different.

Also, as you get more comfortable, pick more complex objects or draw "scenes" like the entire end of the room or, best of all, real people.

Again, don't worry about artistic merit, just keep drawing. Remember, even practicing artists throw away most of their exercise drawings.

However, don't be too surprised if after a few sessions, some of your drawings start to look rather interesting. You may even decide to keep them.

By the way, if you stay with it, you will soon find that you can "doodle" gesture-style drawings and even get in some practice while you are on the phone or stuck in a boring meeting. You may even start drawing the "gesture" your boss is making during his overly long motivational speech.

Adding Color

For ease and convenience you only need pencil and paper to do this exercise. However, if you want to get involved with color, which can only enhance the exercise, here are some simple suggestions.

Use watercolor paints, colored pencils, or colored ink pens. Try adding swatches of color over a completed drawing. Just big swipes, fields of color.

You can restrict them to the interior of your drawing or just wipe the whole page. Let your right brain decide what is most fun.

You can also fill in bits of color between the lines. Turn your piece into a kind of paint-by-number drawing.

Put color wherever you like. You are under no obligation to bow to realism. Your color simply adds an "impression" to your "gesture" drawing.

And finally, remember, it is an exercise. We don't have to like or keep the final product and no one but you need ever see it.

Conversely, if you find you like what your right-side neurons have illogically come up with, then be proud of it. Frame it, show it off, or even sign it and put it up for sale!

Advanced

The advanced exercise involves structure and actual training. Go down to your local university or art school and sign up for a beginning drawing class!

Take a real studio course. Don't worry, you'll find plenty of amateur company. Art classes often contain people just like you who came down to get a little right-brain exercise and experience something different.

You could also just jump right into painting if you think that might tickle your neurons more.

And if you feel you are the more tactile type, how about a sculpture course? What about clay and pottery?

Want to stay close to home? Try model building or wood carving?

The hobby stores are full of projects, all of which will give your right brain a chance to strut its stuff. Remember, any form of pattern copying is right brain exercise. And if you "customize" whatever project you choose, you'll only add to the benefit your brain receives from doing the exercise.

The Sound (and Fury) of Music

Listening to music, particularly instrumental music, engages our right brain in a way most of us find pleasurable (assuming we like the tune).

So every time you listen to a piece of music, that is sit down and really listen, you are getting some good right-brain exercise.

But let's see if we can increase the effectiveness of the exercise, maybe incorporate a few more neural circuits, while still having an enjoyable experience.

Beginner

This one is very simple. But the effect is strong.

For this exercise you will need a recording of some instrumental music. It's best if the music is something new to you, but it isn't a requirement.

Any kind of music will do. You may use popular, ethnic, traditional, classical, whatever you like. You should pick a piece of music that is at least seven minutes in duration but no more than about fifteen. (It's okay to use one movement from a longer piece.)

One restriction only. No singing, no words, just sound.

Words bring the left brain into play and we want to remove it as much as possible for this exercise.

"Heard melodies are sweet, but those unheard
Are sweeter."—Keats

Okay, now find a comfortable spot. Sit or lay down and turn on whatever apparatus you are using to play the music.

Now, close your eyes and at the very beginning of the music imagine the dawn breaking in the eastern sky.

The sun can rise over water, fields, mountains, your choice. The time of year is also whatever you want it to be.

Perhaps the music will suggest a season, even an equatorial region. Let your right brain be your guide here. Just relax and let something come to mind.

Now, as the music plays, imagine the sun rising to its midpoint, then moving across the whole sky, and finally setting in the west.

One entire day will pass. The goal is to have the last rays disappear with the last few bars of music.

Now, first time out, you'll probably get caught in midafternoon, but don't worry. Play the piece again. Keep trying to make a mental synchronization.

And remember to always keep your imaginary view skyward. The horizon can be included, but the sun and sky is your focus.

By the way, the sky can have clouds in it, too. In fact, it could even be so cloudy that the sun nips in and out of view, plays hide and seek. A storm cloud might even pass. You never know till you listen.

Along with everything else, this exercise will probably evoke some fairly strong emotions. If it does, let 'em flow. That's pure right brain!

Repeat the exercise twice more. Do this exercise twice a week for six weeks. After four sessions you may change music if you chose.

Intermediate

This exercise will connect some visual and body control circuits to the auditory ones so that the right side of your brain should really start cooking. (Don't worry, you won't need an ice pack to cool down.)

What we're going to do here is create our own very exclusive, very personalized MTV channel.

Start off by picking out a piece of music that you find interesting and that you have a recording of.

Just as in the beginning section you can use poplar, ethnic, traditional, or classical music, anything you like.

Instrumental music is still preferable, but for this exercise songs with words are okay so long as the words are familiar and evoke strong emotional feelings in you. (This will help to subordinate the logical left-brain circuits that will come into action for the decoding.)

Okay, so find a comfortable place to listen. Use earphones if you like or blast it out on your stereo. For your first session, you should be alone and undisturbed.

Next, locate the album, tape, or CD cover and note how many and what kinds of musicians are going to be playing. If it's a musical group you know, so much the better. You probably have a good idea of what they look like. If not, then you are going to have to use your imagination.

Start the music!

Sit back and close your eyes. Begin to picture each musician in turn playing his or her instrument as the music is rolling. If several are playing at once, focus on one player at a time.

The idea here is to visualize the players as they play. You want to see them with their instruments in hand.

Now give them a little help. Begin to mime the movements yourself as you imagine them being played. (You are, as they say in the business, "doubling").

The goal here is to link the visual and physical with the sound. You want to feel as if the performance is happening in real time and that you are actually contributing to the sound being produced.

Come on, get that rhythm flowing! You've done something like this before. We all have. The only difference here is that we are doing it absolutely purposely. It's great right-brain exercise.

Go through the piece at least two more times. Try to improve your visuals and your timing.

Do this exercise twice a week for six weeks. Use the same piece of music for at least two sessions.

 Advanced exercise requires that you actually play music!

If you already know how to play an instrument, make sure you play it regularly.

If you used to play an instrument, take it up again.

If you have never played an instrument, think about taking a few lessons and starting.

Believe it or not, your brain can learn to play a musical instrument no matter how old you are. It's never too late to start.

Now, you may not achieve virtuoso status or even reach a professional level of performance, but you should have no problem learning how to make organized noise on something.

The choice is wide. Instruments come in all sizes, varieties, and price ranges. There are stringed instruments, wind instruments, keyboard instruments, percussive instruments, even virtual instruments. There are lots and lots of things in the world that can make noise. And if it can make noise, it can be tamed and given a beat!

They even have electronic keyboards for very little money that will fill in most of the notes for you! How easy can it get?

If you're budget is really low, how about a harmonica? You can teach yourself. Just start blowing and sucking. Put on a popular song and dive in, play along. (Just think how cool you'll look, if nothing else.)

However you do it, making music is very good right-brain exercise and also very satisfying.

And if you actually can learn to read music as well, you will be all set to do an important left–right brain crossover exercise.

But for that you have to read Chapter 6!

Some More Fun Right-Brain Exercises

EXERCISE

3

Food and Brain Exercise

The presentation of food on a plate and the layout of the table is an art form in which we have all participated at some time or other. Either we have been guests at a dinner party and therefore part of the composition, or we have cooked and served a meal, becoming the artist. Actually, we've all probably done both.

If you have a penchant for cooking or are simply stuck doing the cooking in your household, here's an excellent chance to do some daily right-brain work.

When you plan your menu, even for an ordinary meal, visualize how the components of that meal will look on the table. Think about it as early as possible. Think aesthetically.

What would look good next to what? Think about the possibility of adding a different color to the mix, perhaps by substituting or adding a vegetable.

Place food on the plates with care and thought.

Not only will you be doing some exercise, but you'll probably get some good reviews as well. Everybody enjoys a good-looking plate of food.

If you don't feel that you can shoulder the pressure of creativity all on your own, check out some cookbooks. The ones with pictures. See what the pros do and copy them. Copying designs is also a right-brain function and good solid exercise.

Don't forget, the pleasurable feeling that you get from eating your food is a right-brain function. Maybe that's why we all enjoy food better when it looks good. We are double-pumping those right-brain neurons!

EXERCISE

4

Puzzling Out Those Pesky Jigsaws

If you like doing jigsaw puzzles, are you in luck! It's a first-rate right-brain exercise. Keep it up. And, to improve the workout, add some background music (if you haven't already).

Also try different types of music to see if you can determine whether or not the type of music you are listening to helps or hinders your concentration.

See if the presence or absence of lyrics and singing affects your spatial processing.

EXERCISE

5

Gallery Visit

Enjoy looking at pictures and sculptures? A visit to the museum will give your right brain plenty of exercise. Just follow these simple guidelines.

Try to go alone or, if you go with someone, separate and meet back later. You don't want any interference with this kind of exercise. It's an exploration that should take place at a comfortable pace. Accommodating a friend breaks the spell and weakens the exercise's potential.

Stand in front of a painting or other work of art and just stare at it for a couple of minutes.

Empty your mind of conscious thought and don't try to figure it out or make sense of it. Just let it wash over you. We're here for exercise, not education or critical evaluation.

Relax your eyes. Let them find their own focus.

Sometimes, especially with impressionism, another dimension appears when your eyes drift and they end up focusing beyond the picture plane in an imaginary background. (That's what makes Claude Monet one of my right brain's favorites. Check out his "Water Lilies" at the Museum of Modern Art in New York City, if you can.)

Okay, if the painting or sculpture doesn't seem to do anything for you, don't worry about it, just move right along. Try the next one. Let your right brain have free reign here. Keep on trying until you find a piece that holds you for inexplicable reasons. If that happens, stare at it as long as your brain wants (or until the museum closes).

The works can be abstract or real, doesn't matter a bit. Whatever your right brain finds intriguing. Remember, no left-brain interference. You can talk about it after it's over or on a return trip.

EXERCISE 6

Ground Plan

This is a map-making or spatial relationship exercise.

Get a piece of paper and a pencil and go into the living room or family room—any big room with lots of stuff in it. Stand against one wall and look toward the opposite wall. Start with the object closest to the far wall. At the top of your paper either write down the name of the object (as in "couch") or do a small outline drawing of the object (a bird's-eye view). Place the name or image on the paper in the same right–left relationship as it is in the room. If the object is nearer to the right wall, put it on the right side of the paper. Nearer the left, put it on the left side. Center, center. You get the idea.

Now, let your eye move to the next object and place it on your paper in the same way. Write down every object in the room (yes, even that pair of sneakers laying on the floor).

You are making a map of the room in plain view! Keep right on going until you get to yourself, then put yourself in the plan.

If you run out of paper, get a bigger piece (or write smaller) and start again. Try to make the spaces between names or objects roughly proportional to the real spaces as you see them.

Now move to the other end of the room and do the same thing.

Map all four views.

Now go lay them out on a table and study them. Do they roughly match up? If not, decide which of the drawings is inaccurate.

On a fresh sheet of paper, draw a rectangle that you think corresponds to the rough dimensions of the room.

Now construct a master plan using the four views as reference. This time use only outline drawings to represent the objects.

Take your finished drawing back into the room, set it down in the center of the room and check to see how you did.

Try another room.

CHAPTER 5

LEFT-BRAIN EXERCISE—LOGIC IS NOT A FOUR-LETTER WORD

"My name is Sherlock Holmes. It is
my business to know what other people don't know."
—Sir Arthur Conan Doyle

The left hemisphere of your brain is known as the "logical" side because it handles, among other things, sequential and logical processing. When we add up numbers, read words off of a page, generate speech, or decode the sounds of language into meaning, we are primarily engaging our left-brain circuits.

That's not to say that the right brain doesn't play a significant part in all of this. Frequently, if not most of the time, the two are working in concert to perform what we think of as "logical" tasks.

Still the right hemisphere must always be a silent partner. That's the reason why it is sometimes referred to as the subconscious (along with the fact that the right side is where dreams and feelings are processed).

Being mute, the right brain most often makes its contribution to problem-solving through a process we call "intuition."

And even when the right brain's contribution is significant, the left brain still gets to claim all the credit. Being able to speak, it is the left brain that presents the "answer" to the world. It can say whatever it wants!

Worse, when the left brain's logic circuit makes a mistake and gives an incorrect answer, it is the right brain that must shoulder the shameful feeling.

In effect, the right brain has to take the blame for the left brain's error.

To quote Rodney Dangerfield, "I tell you life just ain't fair!"

Okay, so even if our left brain is coldly logical and passionless just like the venerable Mr. Spock, we still must rely on it to get us through our daily tasks. Stuff like planning what we're going to do, keeping track of what we've accomplished or not accomplished and, if you're like me, sorting out the big mess you've gotten yourself into by promising too much to too many people.

Therefore, even if we think of ourselves as primarily right-brain oriented, that is to say holistic, highly visual, intuitive, and emotionally sensitive, it is still vital that we keep our sequentially oriented left brain in top shape.

"Everyone prefers belief to the exercise of judgment."
—Seneca

Remember, even an artist can't go very far without intensive use of his or her left brain.

Now obviously the left brain gets a pretty hefty workout in everyday life. But what is more important here is how it is used. If the left brain gets in a rut, relying too heavily on old solutions, we will not be prepared to meet new challenges or emergency situations.

Thinking quickly under pressure taxes our left brain to its limits. So how it performs for us in a crisis is going to be a matter of how prepared it is for action.

We can help it by doing some exercises and also by giving it some new tools to work with. After all, logical processing can be structured in many different ways.

"You can't depend on your judgment when your reasoning power is weak."—Mark Twain

And some of us (we know who we are) have left brains with a tendency to jump on the first solution that comes along and stick to it like glue. We stay with it even if it doesn't work all that well just because, well, that's the way we learned to do it!

Unfortunately, that makes our whole brain think, "Gee, I guess I'm just not very good at that."

Well, it ain't necessarily so.

Exercises

The goal of our left-brain exercise will be to find new ways to use our left-brain circuits more effectively and more reliably. We need to try different approaches to logical thinking that might work better for us. This will help our whole brain feel much more organized and more confident.

EXERCISE 1 — *Deduction: The Ifs, Thens, and Therefores of Logic*

Take scattered or disorganized information, label it, place it into sequential order according to a logical rule, and then deduce a conclusion.

As Sherlock Homes was fond of saying, "Elementary." Well, maybe it was for him because he had a superbly exercised (if somewhat fictitious) brain.

But did you know that there actually was a real brain that provided the model for the way Sherlock Homes did his detective work? It belonged to a medical professor with whom Arthur Conan Doyle studied, a man by the name of Bell. He was legendary for his ability to "deduce" incredible but perfectly logical information about his patients just from simple observation.

Bell performed his deductive pyrotechnics to stress the importance of careful observations in medical diagnosis to his students. It was only inadvertently that he inspired the creation of the greatest detective ever to strut the pages of English literature.

But deductive thinking is not just important to would-be doctors and detectives. We all use this faculty daily. We have to "figure stuff out" pretty much all the time. (For example, I have to constantly deduce where I last put down my glasses.)

Deduction makes very intense use of the brain's logic circuits and is therefore strenuous exercise. We can often "feel the burn" when we are called upon to make use of our basic reasoning skills. Fortunately, it's a pleasurable feeling, otherwise bookstores wouldn't be jammed with detective fiction and they'd never have sold the first copy of the game "Clue."

I think you're already "deducing" that we can easily combine fun with exercise on this one.

Beginner

A simple but effective daily logical deduction exercise is provided at no extra charge in most daily newspapers.

Yes, I'm talking crossword puzzles.

Doing a daily crossword puzzle is excellent left-brain exercise and it's also fun.

Now if you're already an avid crossword puzzler, bravo and move on to the intermediate level. I'm going to be speaking

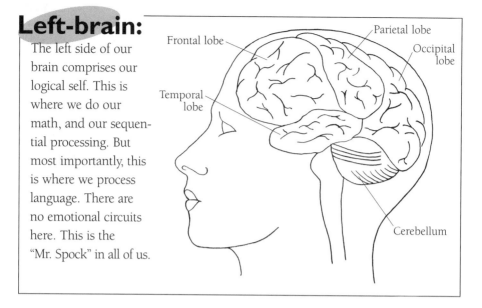

Left-brain:

The left side of our brain comprises our logical self. This is where we do our math, and our sequential processing. But most importantly, this is where we process language. There are no emotional circuits here. This is the "Mr. Spock" in all of us.

Frontal lobe

Temporal lobe

Parietal lobe

Occipital lobe

Cerebellum

here to those among us who find this kind of exercise daunting or frustrating or just plain anxiety-producing.

I'm going to give a beginner lesson in how to approach these sometimes obtuse little critters. They aren't nearly as difficult as they seem.

First of all, remember that for our purposes, it is doing the exercise that counts. There is never a requirement that you finish a crossword puzzle. Doing half or a quarter is fine. Completing the puzzle is something you may want to set for yourself as an eventual goal, but don't worry about it right now.

Okay, start by trying to do the daily puzzle in your local newspaper. In the unlikely event that you find it's too difficult for you to even begin to crack, then start with something simpler.

Any bookstore or library will have books of crossword puzzles of all different levels. Find some puzzles that seem mostly doable for you.

Okay, here's the exercise. Go through the clues and work out as many of the answers as you can. Spend a limited amount of time doing it. Set aside somewhere between fifteen minutes and a half hour, but no more. I don't want you to get frustrated. Stop when you think you've done what you can.

Now, cut out the puzzle and save it.

Even if it's available, don't look at the answers right away. The next day, turn to the answer page and read through both the clues and the answers. Now put the answer sheet away, wait at least fifteen minutes, and take out the unfinished puzzle. Finish up whatever you can still remember. That's it, that's the exercise.

Now, you can do this exercise every day if you like, but being that it is intense, twice a week is just fine. Keep it up for at least six weeks to see some progress.

A Note on Technique

If you are just starting out, you should know a few basic facts about the art of crossword puzzling.

The craft of creating crossword puzzles is idiosyncratic, but all good puzzles are built on a pattern and the pattern can be deduced. That's the challenge and the fun.

Here's a few things to keep in mind.

First of all, almost all puzzles have an overall theme or subject. What that means is that many of answers will be words associated with a given topic, say, for example, names of animals, foods, even movie stars. Keeping the theme in mind often helps.

Also, you should understand that the way the clues are written, the logic of the clues depends entirely on the crossword puzzle creator. Now obviously not every crossword puzzle designer is going to "associate" clues in exactly the same way. They can even have very different ideas on what constitutes a clue. The trick is to try to "think" like the creator, get inside his or her frame of reference.

Another thing you will also notice if you do lots of puzzles is that certain words crop up again and again and seem to be favorites of puzzle designers. In these cases, the designers often stretch the very limits of logic trying to find new clues to disguise frequently used or obvious words.

A final note about ambiguity. Sometimes the clues are purposely designed to be vague and open to multiple interpretations. Be forewarned that any puzzle that offers a prize for a correct completion will undoubtedly have more than one possible solution.

Intermediate

Okay, so you say you're an avid crossword puzzler already. But have you ever tried to create one?

Somebody has to make them up, so why not you?

Wait a minute, here. I though this was supposed to be left-brain exercise? Isn't creativity a right-brain function?

Thinking up clues is deduction in reverse. It's still logic; it's still left-brain. Now, as for making a pattern or a board for your crossword puzzle, that will require some minimal right-brain circuitry. But we're not going to go for an all-out pattern match here. Just a simple grid.

We're going to create a very small, very easy crossword puzzle.

Here's what you do.

First, make a list of ten words. The words can have a theme if you like, but it's not required. Just come up with ten nouns, verbs, adverbs, adjectives, prepositions, whatever you want. If you don't feel creative, grab a book, magazine, or newspaper and just pick some words at random. Be sure to pick words of different lengths. Get at least a couple of biggies in there but don't make them all leviathans either.

Different sizes. And don't worry, you don't have to make a final choice. You can make substitutions any time you want.

Now, for each word, we need to make up a clue. Since we also want to look a little professional here, we need a pattern to our clues. Basically, we need to limit the kinds of associations we use. So we'll do this: The clues must be in the following form. 1. Rhyming. 2. Quote. 3. Location.

To clarify: The clue must either be a sound-alike word, a missing word from a quote (song, poem, well-known phrase), or a place where you would likely find or do whatever the word is.

Okay? So go to it. Write clues for all ten words. As I said, if you have trouble with a word, change it. (Or maybe you see a theme emerging and want to be more consistent.)

All right, when you're finished, pick out the word with the most letters in it and write it down in the middle of a blank piece of paper. (If you want to speed things up, use graph paper and put all the letters inside separate adjoining squares.)

Now, just take another word and find a letter in common. Make your first cross by sharing a letter. Pick another word and stick it on. Don't try to line them up in both directions. It isn't necessary. When you run out of easy connections, put a word somewhere new on the paper and do another cross. You will end up with five groups of two, that's fine. We're not going for complexity here.

Okay, now you have a crossword puzzle. That's it.

If you want to, you can lay a piece of tracing paper on top and make a puzzle blank. Number the squares and black out the squares you aren't using.

You can even test it out on a friend (better be a good one).

This exercise involves letting the puzzle you created in the intermediate exercise grow, just like a little word-garden. (Ah, from humble beginnings!)

Find words that fit and do some interlocking. (A large dictionary comes in very handy here!) Invent clues for the new words as you go, but remember, keep the same association pattern.

If you work on it steadily, you could end up with a pretty good-sized puzzle and might even try submitting it to your local newspaper.

Who knows, you might have just discovered a lucrative side line, or even a new profession! The worst you come away with is some very good deductive exercise.

EXERCISE 2

Fear of Mathematics

Whether we like it or not, our brains process numbers all day long. We live in a society filled with numbers and number systems.

Everybody has an address, which almost always starts with a street number and ends with a zip code.

Most of us also have a telephone number at home and at least one other at our place of work.

Even if we struggled mightily to memorize these all important basic social identification numbers, we can all now recite them just like a mantra.

We positively have to know our address and phone number. And we also need to know our social security number, our bank account number, and God forbid we should forget our ATM code!

Numbers, numbers, everywhere we turn. We can't escape them. Numbers dominate modern life.

Okay, so we're stuck. We have to use those sequencing circuits on the left side of our brain whether we like it or not. Clearly, we need to make sure that they get some regular exercise. But does it have to feel painful, like some kind of mental calisthenics?

Not at all.

The trick is to get the right brain to help out with the problem so that the left brain doesn't have to do all the work. And you know what? Most of us have already unconsciously learned ways to do exactly that.

Let's take a minute and look at how our brains cope with some of the numbers we are forced to use daily.

For example, we tap in our ATM code with our hands in a kind of rhythmic pattern which our right brain readily recognizes. (It helps that the codes are usually only four numbers long.)

We also register a little mental "tune" in our head. Mine goes like this: "TA DA DA TA."

Now, if your right brain is good at picking up patterns, you have probably already guessed that my ATM code has two middle numbers that are the same, and that the first and last numbers are also the same.

(That should give you a pretty big leg up on breaking into my account—and, by the way, those are exactly the kind of clues that professional code breakers earn their living with.)

We do pretty much the same thing with telephone numbers when we're punching them into the keypad.

Ah, but you say this doesn't help at all when someone asks us to tell them the number, does it?

Fortunately, even the phone company knows that seven numbers (ten with the area code) in sequence are just too daunting for the average human brain to cope with.

So they did some studies (hopefully spending a lot of money) and discovered that groups of three and four are okay. The average brain can handle ten digits fine, so long as it's broken up into smaller groups or pattern units.

That's why your local phone number has a dash in it after the first three numbers and why area codes are usually enclosed in parentheses. It's all designed to aide the memory by adding a "pattern" which by definition engages right-brain circuits.

And, of course, the more brain power applied to the problem, the easier it is to do.

So a spoken local telephone number becomes a chant something like this: Dah Dah Dah, (Pause) Dah Dah, Tah, Dah.

Okay, so this is all memory stuff. What does it have to do with sequencing numbers in real time?

Well, the point is that we can use some of the same techniques whenever we have to add, subtract, or even just count.

If we make patterns and set rhythms, we will engage the support of our right brain and therefore make the task easier and much less daunting.

So let's try it.

(Finding a Different Approach)

Beginner

We're going to work with numbers in this exercise, basically just plain old adding up numbers, something we are faced with every day.

Now rather than have you add up a bunch of meaningless numbers which I would have to take the considerable time and trouble to make up and write down, I'm going to ask you to do this exercise when it counts.

The next time you have to figure up your bank account, add up your expenses, or just check over a bill you have received, I want you to put away that cute little calculator you like to use. (Yeah, the one with the environmentally correct solar-power cells.)

In other words, do this exercise whenever you are faced with numbers that must be mathematically manipulated.

Let's start with adding up a column of numbers. Now you were taught in school to start on the right column and work top to bottom adding one number to the next and keeping track of the numbers carried over in your head.

Well, that works fine for very small groups of numbers but when you get a big column, say ten or more numbers, it starts to get uncomfortable, at least for me.

So, here are some different ways to approach it (no, put down that calculator).

Look at the whole column or group of numbers and see what the overall size of the numbers is like.

Are they mostly the same number of digits, or are there a couple of big numbers followed by a lot of little ones?

You see you don't have to approach the column mono-lithically. You could break out some of the numbers into sub groups, pattern them just like the phone company does.

You can do this very simply by making a line under every third number. (Our brain seems love groups of three, don't ask me why.)

You then add up those three number groups individually, then write the result down to the right in a new column. Suddenly that column of fitted numbers becomes a column of five!! Instead of adding down, we are now adding sideways.

The numbers become much easier to see, manipulate, and to double-check.

Another thing we can do is look for complimentary numbers that can be easily combined.

For example, if you see you have a fourteen and a sixteen, well, that's thirty. Cross out fourteen and sixteen and write thirty down.

Despite what you were taught, you don't have to add everything up in order. You can set your own order. Pick out the easy ones to do first, combine them and then make a new column, a smaller column that is easier to handle.

Okay, so we want to look for easy combinations and make new patterns that break the information down into smaller sequences.

Another thing we should always do is a rough estimate. This is stepping back and looking at the whole. Roughly add the numbers, don't worry about accuracy, just round off to the nearest five or ten and see what ballpark you're in. If it's dollars, forget about the cents, or figure only how many dollars they might add. Oftentimes, estimating is all we need to do.

If we are checking a column of numbers where the answer is already given, as when we are presented with a restaurant bill, we can quickly see if the total is reasonable simply by estimating. It may be off by a few cents, but we can quickly tell if a gross error was made. Again, that's often good enough.

Let's move to something a little more complex, multiplication.

Remember sweating out reciting your multiplication tables in front of the whole class? Well, I do. And, after all of that, I came to find out that multiplication is nothing more than adding with offset columns. By the way, I learned this one from an old gaffer accountant way back, when adding machines did exactly that and nothing else.

If you have to multiply two numbers like 402 by 28, here's another way to look at it.

Forget about eight for a moment, you've got 20 × 402s to deal with. That's not so bad. A twenty is just two tens.

(Anybody got change?) Ten times 402 is easy, just add a zero to 402. That gives you 4020. Okay, we need two of them, double it to 8040. Still easy. So far you can do all this in your head, can't you?

Now we still have 8 times 402 left. Well 8 times 400 is fairly easy, that's 3200. So what's left, 2 × 8 or 16. Now you just have to add the three numbers together, which you should still be able to do in your head.

Go on, try it. And no, I'm not going to give you the answer. If you want to check it, go ahead and multiply it out the regular way or, okay, go ahead and get out your fancy electronic calculator.

Now, I'm not trying to get you to start multiplying everything out in your head all the time. I just want you to see that with relatively simple numbers, you can do it. It's kind of fun. So when you are faced with a small multiplication problem, at least do a rough estimate in your head so that the answer will not be a surprise.

Okay, on to counting and reconciling.

The basic idea is the same. Break it down into smaller groups and add a pattern.

"It requires a very unusual mind to undertake the analysis of the obvious."—Alfred N. Whitehead

I once worked as ticket seller in a theater. Every night we had to count all the tickets we had sold and all the tickets we hadn't sold. (This was a pretty big theater so you could grow a beard counting tickets if you didn't know how to speed up the process.)

The method that the box office manager used was wonderful, actually almost an art form.

He would grasp perhaps two hundred tickets at a time. Stack them up like playing cards and then, holding them in one hand, neatly flip through them in a rapid flutter. His fingers were sensitized to feel and he counted each piece of cardboard as it whizzed by. The first time he did this, I was mightily impressed.

But there is a trick of course. He only counted to ten, then imperceptibly ticked the stack so that the counted group was offset. By the time he got to two hundred, he had twenty discrete packs of tickets all laid out in his hand.

The method meant he never counted beyond ten. It also insured that, should he lose count, he only needed to go back ten tickets. Within a few days, I was doing exactly the same thing.

Now I don't expect you to be counting tickets any time soon, but even if you're just doing pennies, the point is the same. Group them; it's faster. And not necessarily even groups, either. For example, with coins it's easier to go in groups of two, then three, two, then three. Why? Add it up, I just counted ten using four motions. It's not only faster, it's easier on the brain.

Same thing when faced with columns of numbers to check. For example, when I reconcile my bank account I am always faced with a column of (I'm embarrassed to say) about twenty ATM withdrawals in amounts ranging from twenty to a hundred dollars. Checking them off one by one always got me in trouble. Even with little pencil marks, somehow I constantly lost my place. Then, finally, I remembered the rule of three. Before I started I would just underline every third number. Now my column of fifteen became five groups. I did my checking in threes and suddenly I was a whiz.

Remember, sequential does not mean in order. It just means one after the other. But you can chose which comes first, second, and third, and you can process sequences in groups and patterns. We're just all programmed to accept the sequence we are given without thinking that there might be a better way.

Your left brain can come up with wonderfully creative solutions to sequential processing, if only you will let it.

So what's the exercise, you ask? The exercise is to try to think of different ways to do what you already do. The next time you are faced with some numbers, try working with them differently and, if you can, completely in your head. You'll find it will change the way you think and wake up some long-dormant neurons. (By the way, does anyone still remember eight times nine?)

Intermediate to Advanced

········▶ I have only mentioned a very few mathematical tricks here. But there are many excellent books on tricks and techniques for math and number skills if you feel your brain needs some freshening in this area. Go find some of these books and work through them. You may find that numbers aren't daunting after all. In fact, they can be intriguing.

Speaking of which, a book on code making and breaking is also a great place to find some heavy-duty left-brain puzzles to solve. Codes are becoming more and more a part of our life. Perhaps your brain might like to find out a little more about this subject.

Some More Fun Left-Brain Exercises

EXERCISE

3

Computer Programming

We all understand that computers are logic machines. They execute logical instructions in exact sequential order, exactly as they are told to do.

So, naturally, programming a computer requires intensive use of the brain's logical thought circuits. In order to get the computer to do what you want it to do, you must break the task down into simple logical steps and then assemble those steps sequentially.

Sound like good left-brain exercise? You bet, probably as good as it gets.

Any time you engage in programming at any level you are doing some great left-brain exercise. And for you sane people who know better than to mess with binary and hexadecimal numbers, take heart in this fact: just learning to operate a computer program relies heavily on your left-brain circuits.

Whether it's laying out a letter template on your word processor or doing your finances on a spreadsheet or even manipulating images on a graphics program, it heavily involves your left brain.

All that stuff that you have to do to get something to happen is great for your left brain.

Why? Because the computer does exactly what you tell it to do. I know, I know. But even when it seems to have a mind of its own, it is merely trying to do what you told it to do. You have just made some subtle logical error, which you have to backtrack and find using your own logic circuits.

The exception also proves the rule. When there is a "bug" in the program, that means that there was a logical mistake made by some faceless programmer back there at whoosie-soft.

You discover the error by determining, precisely, that *your* logic is faultless. Ergo, the program must be faulty. Wow! That's some terrific left-brain exercise and, yes, I hate it, too.

But next time you are deep in the throes of a maddening computer glitch, take some consolation in the fact that although your nervous system is teetering on the brink of meltdown, you are doing absolutely super things for your left brain!

Games of Strategy and Logic

Notice I didn't mention computer games as left-brain exercise. That's because most of them are some form of shoot 'em up. But if the game involves lots of logical thinking, planning, deducing, and a minimum of upper cuts, then it qualifies as left-brain exercise.

And if you can tear yourself away from those glowing phosphors for a few hours, there are lots of old-fashioned games that make heavy use of logic.

For more on this subject, turn to the Chapter 14 "The Games We Play."

Left-Brain Reading

Reading is a obviously good left-brain exercise, especially informational reading. Reading stories and fiction, while of course using the left brain, tend to kick in those right-brain image and imagination circuits. It's actually more of a crossover exercise.

But informational reading stresses the left brain, especially highly technical reading. That's one of the reasons it seems "harder." It's because you are getting very little help from your right brain.

Now if you need to read lots of technical information for school or work and are having trouble doing it, turn to the end of Chapter 6 on right–left brain exercises for some tips on how to get your right brain to help out a little, or maybe even a lot.

AN EQUAL PARTNERSHIP MAKES FOR CREATIVE THINKING

"Einstein's space is no closer to reality than Van Gogh's sky."—Arthur Koestler

Exercises To Keep the Two Halves Whole

Suddenly a problem crops up and our trusty brain swings into action to resolve it.

Most of the time, if we persevere, our brain will come up with some sort of mundane but practical solution. Problem solved, no big deal.

But every once in a while our brain seems to surprise us and come up with a really good idea, something novel and innovative that wows everyone including ourselves.

We secretly shout "I'm a genius!" And we seem to be, at least for the moment.

But then another problem arises and our brilliance somehow fades and we're back to our ordinary uncreative self. How come?

And how come some people seem to come up with creative ideas consistently? Is it something to do with being really smart?

Not at all. Studies of highly creative people in both the arts and the sciences have revealed that native intelligence actually has little to do with the process. Some creative people are very smart, some average, a few are even below average.

Creativity is apparently not a function of intelligence.

In fact, just about the only thing that highly creative people seem to have in common is an easy and harmonious flow of information between the right- and left-brain hemispheres. It seems that during the creative process, both halves of the brain focus on the problem. It's a shared effort, or at least it's suppose to be.

In a kind of parody of the old saying "two heads are better than one," it appears that what is actually true, when it comes to creativity, is that two half brains working together are better than one (half). And this holds true for both the arts and the sciences.

"First and last, what is demanded of genius is love of truth."—Goethe

Albert Einstein "discovered" the theory of relativity without performing a single scientific experiment. In fact, the only tool he used was his creativity. He simply imagined what it would be like to take a ride on a beam of light. He let his right brain call up a visual image while his left brain carefully examined what he would actually be able to see. From this "thought experiment," as he liked to call it, he was able to "deduce" basic laws of nature.

And it may interest you to know that Einstein did his science with a brain that he himself felt was not dissimilar to that of an artist.

Okay, maybe none of us are quite as creative as old Albert was, but we can all increase our creativity by increasing the flow between the two brain hemispheres. All we have to do are some exercises that require the two halves of the brain to work together.

Better communication and better coordination are the keys to freeing up our creative potential and, incidentally, to making our brain feel fresh and vigorous.

You'll find this type of exercise is a kind of brain Aerobics. It really gets those synaptic signals pumping and makes you feel great!

The Exercises

Lots of things we do require both halves of our brain to work at the same time. But working together is another matter.

For example, many of us like to listen to music while we are working on a task that largely employs our left brain, such as organizing or writing or logical problem-solving.

But the two tasks are not coordinated. Although it is certainly pleasing to have the music on, if you notice carefully, as soon as the problem becomes difficult and you kick your logical brain circuits into high gear, the music will fade into the background. In fact, you may no longer perceive it all. Your brain filters it out because it is, in this case, distracting.

"Thinking is a momentary dismissal of irrelevancies."
—R. Buckminster Fuller

Watching a motion picture also uses both sides of the brain because we are listening to people talk while viewing pictures.

But this is hardly a very taxing exercise, unless, oddly enough, the sound quality is so poor that we must coordinate the visual lip movements of the actors with the mangled words we are hearing in order to rescue meaning.

Reasonably good exercise, but not much fun and not terribly easy to arrange. You can't very well go to your local theater and say to the projectionists "Could you garble the sound a little, please? I'm trying to get a little right–left-brain exercise."

But not to worry, the exercises below should do the trick.

Say It With Feeling

Beginner

➤ One of the simplest ways to get the two halves of the brain working on the same page is to read the page out loud!

When I was in elementary school I once had a teacher who made us "recite" a poem in front of the class every two weeks. We were graded on how forcefully we delivered our verse. That is to say, how much "dramatic" interpretation we added to the recitation.

That teacher probably didn't know that reading words out loud while attempting to interpret and impart their emotional content requires a feat of left–right-brain coordination. But she certainly did know a good brain exercise when she saw one.

Okay, so choose anything you like: a poem, a story, an essay, even a speech to rally the troops at the office—anything, just so long as it has some dramatic potential.

Now, find yourself a nice private, soundproof spot and sing it out with as much feeling as you can muster. I give you full permission to thunder, roar, and generally emote. And don't feel self-conscious about your perhaps limited thespian potential. We're not expecting you to go in front of a live audience and wow them as I had to do in sixth grade. (Unless of course you actually harbor some secret desire to tread the boards—in which case you may want to refer to the exercises professional actors use in Chapter 12.)

Creativity:

In creative people there is an easy and free flow of information across a bridge between the two brain hemispheres known as the corpus callosum.

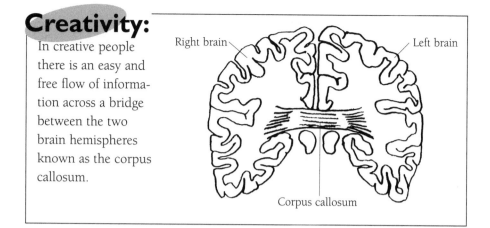

Right brain

Left brain

Corpus callosum

The main point here is to use your emotional circuits in coordination with your language circuits. (If you're shy, this may also turn out to be a confidence booster.)

Read aloud at least one full page, more if you like.

Read through the material at least three times per session attempting each time to hone the meaning a little finer. The interpretation is your own of course, but do your best to stay true to the meaning of the words. Try to comprehend the author's intention. And, by the way, the author can be you. Feel free to read your own work out loud if you like.

Do this exercise at least twice a week for six weeks.

Note that while memorization is not required for this exercise, it certainly would be a way to combine two exercises in one! Think about trying it.

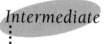

Intermediate

A very good and fun way to increase the difficulty of the exercise is to move from dramatic speech to full singing. That's right; sing a song. Music increases the complexity by bringing in the element of tone and rhythm. It becomes, as they say, a qusetion of timing.

Now if you feel you just can't a carry a tune, even in a bucket, not to worry. Chanting is almost as good. Nowadays I believe it is popularly known as "rapping," but trust me, the

Gregorians were doing it long before Snoop Doggy Dog or Ice-T signed their first multi-million dollar record deal. Chanting is probably as old as pounding hollow tree trunks with ox bones, if not a whole lot older.

Chanting or singing, singly or in groups, is very good left–right-brain coordination exercise.

You can even sing along with a favorite record or, better yet, find a Japanese-style karaoke recording. That's music minus one. It's a recording of the instrumental and backup parts of a song with the solo singer left out. You get to be that solo singer!

It's all the rage in Japan. They even have special clubs that let you get up on stage and become a "live" performer. None of that wimpy American-style lip synching here.

Okay, you aren't required to make a public debut, but do engage in either singing or chanting on a regular basis. You may even want to check out the possibility of taking some singing lessons. You could meet with your local church choir director for advice. You may find out that you don't sound all that bad, and it's terrific brain exercise, as well as a lot of fun

By the way, if you play an instrument, so much the better. Play and sing at the same time. Great exercise.

Advanced

One of the best exercises to help the flow between the two brains is sight-reading music. Naturally this requires that you both play an instrument and read music.

If you don't do either, think about learning. It's never too late. You can easily find qualified musicians willing to give you lessons in the instrument of your choice. Just check the classified ads in your newspapers or the yellow pages. Always wanted to take up the guitar or piano? Now's your chance.

And if you want simplicity itself, take up the recorder. It's inexpensive and easy. You can even teach yourself. The recorder is a small flute usually made of wood but available for less money in plastic. It is easy to play and is often used to teach people how to read music. You can find a beginner book at almost any music store and even without a teacher, pick it up quickly.

You can also, of course, sight-read with your own voice at no charge. But if you want some very good advanced exercise, find some music that you don't already know and read through it.

Some Other Good Left-Right Exercises

EXERCISE

2

Real Time Problem Solving

Anytime you are faced with a complex problem or plan, you have an excellent opportunity to engage in an important left–right-brain interaction. One that will not only exercise and improve your brain, but actually help you solve the problem or make the plan quicker and easier.

You've probably heard it said that we don't use the full capability of our brains. Well, when it comes to problem solving, most of us are letting half of our brain stand idly by, simply because we don't understand how to usefully engage it.

"The universe is change;
our life is what our thoughts make it."
—Marcus Aurelius

So the next time you sit down to think through a problem or make a plan, don't just fire up those logic and sequential circuits. Get some help from your right brain. If you will just allow it to join in on the problem solving, it can make its considerable processing power felt—to very useful effect.

How do you do this?

Very simply; in fact you probably already do some of this instinctively. I'm just going to clarify the process so that you can take full advantage of it.

When thinking over a problem, always have some paper and a pencil handy. Now besides just writing down the elements of the problem or perhaps outlining the plan sequentially, try to find some way to turn the problem or plan into a visual. By which I mean make diagrams, symbols, maps. Draw some kind of a picture. The act of drawing directly engages the right brain as does the stimulation of looking at the images. In addition, try to "picture" the problem in your mind if you can.

You see, the real strength of the right brain is overall unification. The right brain can take in the whole problem or plan all at once, if you will just let it.

You do this by visualizing the so-called "big picture." Just try to step back from the problem mentally and see the larger perspective, the larger implications, the overall dimensions.

That is what the "big picture" is all about and people that are valued have the ability to quickly grasp this larger view. They see consequences and implications far more clearly than others because they successfully engage their right-brain visualization circuits while the rest of us are only using our left-brain logic circuits. No wonder they have an advantage.

So, in a very real sense, what I am telling you is to open up your mind, use your whole brain. Find ways to get that right brain fired up and you will be surprised at how much quicker and easier problem-solving becomes.

By the way, the very same is true in reverse. Those problems that are mostly right brain—usually artistic or graphic in nature—can benefit from the addition of left-brain circuitry. Here you try to sequentialize the problem.

Write things down in lists. Procedures, steps, timings, materials. Add a practical approach to the problem. Put your logic circuits on the case.

Doing these seemingly simple things greatly improves your brain's functional ability. Remember, you will be doubling your capability with very little additional effort.

EXERCISE
3

Creative writing

Writing stories, essays, poems, or just keeping a journal requires that your left and right brain work in concert. It's particularly effective exercise when you engage in visually descriptive writing.

If you are uncomfortable with the idea of making up a story, simply tell a story you know. Dramatize a story you heard, some event that you participated in, or combine the two. Try to think visually and describe what you saw, what happened, what was said.

Remember this is an exercise so you don't have to show anyone what you have written down, or even keep it. The doing is the exercise.

EXERCISE
4

Whistle While You Work (or Jog)

Whistling, singing, or chanting while doing a simple or repetitive manual task seems to help the brain stay focused and, therefore, more effectively control the body's movements.

As we all know, if the brain isn't fully engaged, it will find things to do. It will wander off idly like a small child. If you happen to be engaged in something serious like swinging an ax, well, better not to contemplate.

Staying focused when doing something physical that requires very little brain power is always a problem. Even if you are just taking your morning jog, the chance of a misstep and a turned ankle might just be lessened by engaging your mind in some form or rhythmic harmony that mirrors the exercise and keeps you thinking about the old "left-right-left."

It also seems to make the time pass faster and keeps your brain from asking the all-important question, "why the hell am I doing this?"

A busy brain has no time for foolish introspection. Perhaps this explains the military's fondness for making new recruits "sound off" while they are being driven to the limits of physical endurance.

So if you are faced with some boring task, physical or otherwise, and you have no friendly drill sergeant to set the cadence for you, try keeping your brain fully engaged with some appropriate musical or rhythmic exercise.

Just make sure it doesn't interfere with your concentration or become a safety issue.

EXERCISE

5

Computers Again!

Remember when personal computers first came out and all you had in the way of an interface was a command line? Then along came the Graphic User Interface, Apple's Macintosh, and later Microsoft's Windows. Everybody found the pictorial and colorful GUI interface so much easier to use. Why?

You guessed it, because it finally let the right brain in on what had been a purely left-brain enterprise. And, as we have learned, letting the two sides work together is faster, easier, and just plain better.

Whenever you work on a computer, providing it has a Graphic User Interface, you are doing crossover left–right-brain exercises. The ease of using a mouse to click on a little pictorial symbol of what you want to do, versus memorizing a series of arcane and unintuitive keystrokes should convince you that, indeed, two brains are better than one.

Remember, always try to incorporate both hemispheres of your brain whenever you can in whatever you do.

EXERCISE

6

Crossover Reading

Whenever you are reading some kind of story, fiction, biography, or even just a newspaper account of, say, a crime, you are engaging not only your left-brain reading circuits but also your right-brain visualization circuits. You are making a picture in your head using the words as cues. The early filmmaker D. W. Griffith even went so far as to say that he learned his craft from Charles Dickens.

So enjoy those novels and stories and keep on creating those images in your right brain. It's a good crossover exercise.

By the way, for those times when you are stuck plowing though highly technical information that more or less isolates you in left-brain mode, here's a tip. Bring in your right-brain circuits to help out. How?

Visualize the information as much as you can. Make little drawings in the margin or on a separate piece of paper. If the technical writer is good, he or she will include as many diagrams as possible for exactly this reason. But even when the publisher is too cheap to include them, you can help yourself by making the diagrams yourself. It will greatly help you to visualize and that kicks in the right side. Now we're firing on two cylinders instead of one. Makes a big difference.

CHAPTER 7

VISUALIZATION: THE KEY TO REALIZATION

How To Widen Your Vision and Expand Your Horizons

Visualization is one of the most important brain systems we possess and one that we should make sure is in top shape at all times.

This is the famous "mind's eye," that part of our brain that lets us see objects and events outside of real time. It allows us to recall things visually, things that have already transpired and it makes it possible to imagine things the way they *might be* or *will be* in the future.

It's amazing when you think about it. We humans can actually "see" the future in our mind's eye. It's the key to our imagination and the foundation of our creativity. In fact, just try to "imagine" doing anything without first visualizing it!

For example, just try to find your lost car in a parking lot without being able to mentally picture what it looks like. Ah, you have that problem, do you? See, you do need some exercise. And, by the way, exercise will definitely help.

Many of us think that only people like artists or architects are born with highly developed visualization systems, and that the rest of us are a bunch of semi-blind dullards, stuck with inferior internal vision. Well, it simply ain't so.

We all have this ability and we all can develop it to a very high degree.

Not only does an architect "see" a building before it is built, but an entrepreneur "sees" his or her product before it realized. A baseball pitcher "sees" himself throwing the ball perfectly just over the outside corner while at the same time the hitter "sees" himself knocking the ball over the outfield fence. We all see ourselves doing things before we actually do them.

"If a man take no thought at what is distant,
he will find sorrow near at hand."—Confucius

Visualization is a key process in all human endeavors. It's how we convince ourselves that we can succeed. Successful people see themselves doing things that other people tell them can't be done.

The art of Zen makes a religious discipline out of this ability. Zen masters believe that the mind's eye sees much more clearly than the external eyes. Learning to trust and rely on the internal eye is one of the goals of Zen. Here's a story that illustrates what they mean.

A famous Zen archer once amazed a student by stepping out into a pitch-dark, moonless night to demonstrate how to shoot an arrow into a target using only the mind's eye.

Although the archer could see nothing in the blackness, he told his brain to "visualize" the target that he knew was out there in the dark some forty paces from his house.

Since he had fired at that same target many times in the daylight, his mind's eye indeed could visualize the distance and range.

All the Archer needed to do was to trust his mind's eye. And so confident was the Archer that after he fired the arrow into the night he simply walked back into the house declaring to the student that he had hit the center.

The student, of course, stumbled out into the field, searching blindly with his arms outstretched until he was able to locate the target. Feeling with his hands, he discovered the arrow dead center, as the archer had said. This is a true story and what the archer was able to do was not magic.

Although the Zen archer could not see the target, he knew for a fact that the target was there in the exact spot that he could "visualize." Eventually, his student was able to duplicate the feat, because improving the skill of visualization is just a matter of practice.

It's an ability that all humans share and one that is far too valuable to allow to deteriorate. Remember playing "Pin the Tail on the Donkey" and "Blind Man's Bluff" as a child? Well guess what, those were visualization exercises disguised as games. Now what do you say we try some adult versions?

Of course, if you prefer, you can still pick up a couple of artificial donkey tails and a blindfold at your local toy store.

Exercises

EXERCISE **1**

Beginner

Re-Visualization

▶ *Picture What You Already Know Is There*

This is a simple exercise that, with repetition, will sharpen your ability to visualize familiar objects.

Assuming you are at home for this exercise, find a comfortable space to sit that has an uncluttered view. A blank wall is good. If you have no blank wall, try laying down and looking up at the ceiling. You may also just close your eyes if you are comfortable doing so.

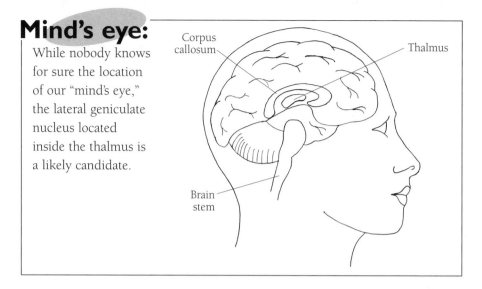

Mind's eye:
While nobody knows for sure the location of our "mind's eye," the lateral geniculate nucleus located inside the thalmus is a likely candidate.

Now, picture your workspace in your mind. For example, let's say you're an office worker. You're going to mentally picture your desk as you last saw it and as you expect to see it next time you go to the office.

The first thing you want to do is to set your point of view. Start by imagining that you are standing several feet away, behind your desk. The view is one you have seen before. It's how you approach your desk to sit down when you arrive. The lighting in the room or office is as it would be in the morning.

Now, imagine you are standing, looking slightly down at your desk. Just try to picture the basic shape. See the chair in front of it, the drawer fronts and, if they are visible, the legs.

There's probably some stuff on top. Maybe a computer and some books or papers. They can all just be rough shapes right now, don't worry too much about full detail yet. See the overall picture. Move your head from side to side to see how that changes the view. Lift your head slightly. See the walls on either side and then study the background. See what's there; maybe a bulletin board, a calendar, a picture, or even just a smoothly painted wall, a window, a door. Whatever you know is there, see it. Look up briefly at the ceiling. Note the position of the lights and the air flow ducts or sprinkler heads. See that the lights are on.

Now take a step toward the desk. Picture yourself walking toward your desk just as you do in the morning. Pull out the chair and sit down. Put your hands on your desk, palms down. Look at your hands.

Now, moving your attention from your hands, look at the objects on the desk. What is near your left hand? A computer monitor? Personal pictures? Papers? Pencil cup? What is near your right hand? Telephone? Day calendar? Reference books? Visualize touching the phone receiver. Pick it up and dial your home number. See the dial pad. Watch your hand key in the numbers.

Now put the receiver back in the cradle. Move back in your chair and pull out a drawer. Get something out, lay it on the desk.

If you like to explore, visualize a few other objects; pick them up, put them down. Remember to visualize your hands doing the task. It is very important to incorporate yourself, that is your body, into the exercise.

Placing your hands in the frame helps make it more real for your mind. It allows tactile triggers to aid in the revisualization process.

Finish your session by pushing away from your desk and standing up. Take one more look down at your desk, turn around, and close your eyes.

Now tilt your head down, open your eyes and look at your real body (your lap if you have been sitting). The exercise is now over.

I want to note that this is not intended as a memory exercise even though it certainly engages the memory circuits fairly heavily. What is important here is image, not certitude, and not completeness. Detailed visual images come with practice.

> *"The test of a first-rate intelligence is the ability to hold two opposed ideas in the mind at the same time, and still retain the ability to function."*
> *—F. Scott Fitzgerald*

If all you see and touch right now is vague forms, don't worry. That is more than enough for your first couple of sessions. In fact, the first time you do this exercise you will probably leave out some very large prominent objects. Don't worry about it. The point here is to get started.

If you don't work in an office, just modify the exercise to fit the space in which you actually do work.

And if you really hate your job and don't want to be there at all, even in your mind, this exercise can also be done using your home or apartment.

Just pick a room you do something specific in, like the kitchen. Stand in front of the sink and visually go though it, getting out what you need to make coffee or a simple meal. Turn around and examine the stove, the refrigerator, anything you like.

The garage or home workspace is another possibility. Remember somewhere that you perform specific tasks and store equipment to carry out that task.

Do try, however, to be out of the room in question for at least a couple of hours before doing this exercise.

Stay with this exercise at least a good fifteen minutes per session, longer if you like. Try to repeat the same exercise at least twice a week for six weeks. After that, move to a different location if you like.

Intermediate

Although the basic form of the exercise is all you really need, you can increase the difficulty by visualizing a full and complete process from beginning to end.

Take some task you do regularly and must do sometime soon. A good one is putting the groceries away.

Imagine what you need to buy the next time you go to the store. Now put yourself in the kitchen, coming back from the store with the bag. Unload it on the counter and go through the items. Visualize them as you pick them up one by one and put them where they belong. Remember to see your hands as they grasp and hold the objects. End by folding up and putting away the bag.

You'll quickly realize that we already do this kind of exercise every time we are faced with a task we have done before. We very naturally try to visualize what we are going to do before we do it. It's how we prepare and plan. Here, in this exercise, we are just making it more conscious, more deliberate, so that when we do it for real, that is, unconsciously, we will have a sharper focus.

By the way, another good one to practice is what your car looks like. Yes, spend a little time each day picturing it from all four sides. (And don't forget to see all the little dents and imperfections that make your car unique.) Try opening and closing the doors, the truck, and the hood.

This is the original version of virtual reality, the one we've done for centuries without the aid of computers.

Take a visual mind trip. Walk down to the store or drive your car somewhere around town. Picture every corner, every traffic light, every landmark along the way as you come upon it.

If you decide to stop and enter a store, picture opening the door. Look to see where the counter is, where the shopping aisles are.

Go get something specific off one of the shelves, some product you know well. Examine the packaging, make sure it's sealed (safety first).

Carry it back to the checkout aisle. Move it around in your hand as you walk and feel the size and weight as you look at it. Be careful not to run into the other shoppers. You do see them, don't you?

I think you get the idea here.

Another good advanced exercise involves the use of a map of your city, town, or neighborhood.

Lay the map out in front of you. Randomly point to intersections with a pencil. Now picture in your mind what that intersection looks like. What's on each corner? Try to picture driving or walking up to it the way you most commonly approach it. Stop in the middle and mentally look to the four compass points one at a time. What do you see? What time of day is it? Where's the sun? Do this for a minimum of five locations.

These advanced exercises need only be done once a week.

Both of these exercises are intense, but if you chose to do them, they will really sharpen up your visualization circuits. If you really enjoy doing them, you a might make a good candidate for a motion picture director.

Things as They're Not!

2

Beginner

▶ This exercise is about training our visualization system to "see" possibilities, not just realities.

If you can, you should do this exercise, at least initially, in your own home or apartment. The room you choose should be a large, social room, one that has furniture in it— a couch, chairs, coffee tables—such as the living room, family room, or den.

Place yourself somewhere that commands an overall view of the entire room. For example, stand in a corner against the wall or in a doorway. Somewhere you can see the room without being too much in the room.

You may bring in a chair from outside the room if you feel more comfortable sitting down. Don't use a chair from the room.

Once the exercise is underway and you have your task firmly pictured in you mind, you may move around the room in order to visualize it from different angles.

Okay, now start by examining a large object.

A couch is ideal, but a stuffed chair, a desk, or even a table will serve. Just so long as it is fairly massive; it should be as big or bigger than you.

Look it over carefully until you have burned the image into your mind's eye—its shape, its width, its bulk. Close your eyes and picture the object for a moment. Now open them and look at it again. Repeat this a couple of times until you can hold some detail.

When you look with your eyes closed, at first they'll be some vague or indistinct areas. That's okay. Open your eyes and reexamine those areas specifically. Do your best, but don't worry that you can't immediately form a perfect image. That's why we're doing the exercise.

Next, look around the room and find an empty space to put the object in.

Yes, we're playing interior decorator, only we aren't concerned here with aesthetics.

We don't care in the least how practical the new location is. All we care about is that, in our estimation, it will actually fit. (By the way, feel free to mentally rotate the object if necessary.)

Now, hocus pocus, move the object!

Making sure the actual object is no longer in your field of view, picture in your mind the object in its new location. Look at how it fits into the background. See how much floor space it consumes. Walk around it and examine it to see if you have enough room to do so. You may have to squeeze between it and the wall, but that's even more interesting.

Now move the object again. Try it several other places if you have room. Continue until you have no more places to put it.

When you have exhausted the possibilities, pick out another object to move. Only this time make it something small. Something that sits on top of something else, like a lamp, a vase, or a keepsake.

Try moving it to a new location on top of something else, maybe the mantle or another coffee table, or just plop it down on a cushion on the couch. You can even set it down on the floor, over in the corner or right in the middle of the rug.

(Hint: Sometimes the more bizarre the location, the easier it is to see!)

Spend at least fifteen minutes on this exercise and don't worry about how clearly you see the first few times. With practice, you will get much better.

You should do this exercise at least twice a week for six weeks.

Okay, we're going to do a variation on the earlier exercise. We are going to try and move more than one object at a time. We are going to combine moves.

For example, take the couch and shove it over against the wall and then put a chair or coffee table right on top of it the way you would if you were planning to clear the floor space. Stack things up! Picture everything in the room, stacked up tightly against the walls with the center parts of the room absolutely clear.

Concentrate on viewing the room, not the furniture. Notice the increase in space. Now make all that furniture you shoved up against the wall disappear! Empty the room!

Pretend it's moving day if you like. The workmen have just cleared out the last object. (If you have a memory of the room when you first moved in, use it to help you.)

Notice how much bigger the room has gotten. Look at how the color of the wall has become more intense now that it's fully exposed.

Now we're going to have some real fun. We're going to repaint those bare walls with some really bright colors! Yeah, wild colors, nothing timid here. We're going for Technicolor.

Start with bright red. It's an easy color to visualize. We're going to imagine painting the walls fire-engine red. Hey, hey, don't worry, we'll paint it out before anybody else sees it. No one will ever know!

Okay, now try bright, bright yellow, then orange, then green.

Use saturated colors so you can really notice how the doors and windows stand out. (Don't paint them and don't paint the ceiling, leave it white or whatever color it was.)

After your initial session, vary the shades if you like and you may even use a color chart or sample to aid you. You can get them at a paint store, usually at no charge.

Now, of course, you really are playing interior decorator and you will be doing exactly the same thing the good ones do when the pick color for a room. They try to "see" it.

Oh, and don't be too surprised if you end up with a strong urge to repaint the room. Sorry about that.

Try this exercise once a week for six weeks. Change rooms as often as you like. And, yes, you can just stay with a basic palette of primary colors.

There is no requirement to visualize designer colors like Spring Morning Yellow or Saddle-Boot Maroon.

Advanced

For this exercise we are going to try to look into the past, at the way things were. No, not nostalgia, reality.

For this exercise we are going to be either outdoors or by a window that gives us a fairly good vista. We need to see into the distance and we need to see some buildings.

Okay, the easiest way to do this is to go outside, moving a hundred feet or so away from your house if you can. Walk down to the corner or into the backyard and stand against the far fence looking back toward the house.

Now imagine the scene in front of you without your house. Make it disappear and visualize the view with your house gone. Leave the other houses if you live on a block with several houses, just turn your house into the vacant lot that it once was. Suddenly there's a void. From where you stand, you can now see through to the house across the street or to the yard behind your house. The street is there, even the driveway, but no house!

Now imagine grass or wildflowers or even just weeds growing where your house will one day stand.

Imagine a tree, a large tree soaring up above where your roof line used to be. Look way above your house and see the branches sway as the wind catches them. Now follow the branches back down the trunk, right through where your house will one day be. Look down to the massive base of the tree.

There is some kind of animal laying there, maybe a cow or a deer or even just a lazy dog. It's resting under the tree. It's staring at you, curious as to what you are doing. Don't worry, it's not threatening.

Move closer, within twenty-five feet or so of your house.

Okay, now they're coming to build your house. Suddenly the tree is gone. The ground is opened up, raw dirt is exposed. They've graded! There's a pile of dirt off to the side, left over from the foundation work. (A truck is going to come to take it away.)

In the front yard there is a big pile of building materials covered by a tarp. If your house is brick, there's a big pile of bricks. If it's wood, a neatly stacked pile of wood.

You're looking at just the foundation now. You see the outline of all the rooms, but no building. You see raw floors but no walls. Examine the foundation carefully, study how the rooms are going to look once the walls are up. Pace them off by walking around the whole house if you like.

"A man's own observation, what he finds good of and what he finds hurt of, is the best physic to preserve health."—Francis Bacon

Okay, now go back inside the house, but remember, there are still no exterior or interior walls. They haven't been built yet.

Now try to picture all of your furniture sitting on this new floor. Your couch, your television, your bed, your bookcases, your dining room or kitchen table.

There it all is, everything you own, open to the elements! (Gee, I hope it doesn't rain.)

Stand in front of one of these walls-to-be and see through it to the furniture in the next room.

Visualize each room with furniture but no walls.

See if you can visualize something unusual about the arrangement, something you won't be able to see once the walls are up.

For example, the relationship of furniture from one room to the next. Did you realize that your living room couch was actually only a foot away from the headboard of your bed? Now you can notice such odd things.

Walk through the house. Stay on the floor plan. Even though the walls aren't there, we're going to respect their boundaries. Pretend to open doors that we know aren't there yet.

Study different views. Each time you go in a room, look through to the next room, then if there's another, to it and so on until you get to the exterior wall. Then look beyond that to the yard.

See everything that you can. When you move from one room to the next, notice what you forgot or didn't see and note it for next time. If you like, go back to the previous room and look at it again, this time with the forgotten objects in place.

Stay with this exercise as long as it interests you to do so.

You can leave off at any point and pick it up later if you like. And you can repeat this exercise often.

You probably won't run out of things to correct and adjust but if you do, then you have succeeded. Your visualization powers are now in top shape!

Architects do a variation of this exercise when they actually try to imagine their projects in the field, both before and during construction.

3

Zen Archery Revealed!

And, finally, for those of you who found the story of the Zen archer intriguing, yes, I'm going to give you an exercise to put you on the road to doing exactly what he did!

Arrows being a bit dangerous, I will suggest a gentler alternative. Get a hold of some tennis balls or baseballs or just plain rubber balls, whatever you like, but get several.

You must have at least three, and they must be as nearly identical as possible. It's very important that they at least "feel" the same.

Now get yourself a one- or two-gallon bucket of some sort. Basically something to pitch the balls into. Doesn't matter what it is, so long as it can trap the balls thrown into it and it is something you can use again and again.

Put the bucket or trap on the ground. (The location can be inside or outside. If it's inside just make sure that there isn't anything breakable nearby.)

Now stand about seven to ten feet away. No further, no closer.

Okay, begin by simply pitching the balls toward the target, underhanded. Throw three balls one at a time, then retrieve them, and repeat.

Establish a regular pitching motion. It doesn't matter what your style is, as long as you do it the same way, over and over again.

Now, keep doing this until you can fairly consistently get the balls in the bucket. This may take you several sessions or you could be a natural and pitch them right in. If you find you are having trouble, keep moving closer until you can hit the target. (Distance is not what we're after right now.)

Now that you feel pretty good about getting the balls in most of the time, you are ready to "visualize."

Throw a ball in the bucket. If you miss, retrieve the ball, do not use your second or third one. Keep going till you get it in.

Now take another ball and get ready to throw. Look at the bucket carefully and close your eyes. Picture the bucket in your mind's eye. Go ahead and pitch the ball toward the bucket. With your eyes still closed, watch the ball leave your hand, arc up in the air and come down in the bucket.

If you miss, immediately open your eyes and try to pick up where the ball actually went, long or short, to the right or left side, whatever. Now close your eyes again and see the ball going astray. Correct your throw. With your eyes still closed and the third ball in your hand, go through your throwing motion without releasing the ball. Feel and see the correction.

Open your eyes and take one more look at the bucket. Close your eyes again and pitch the ball.

If you miss again, keep practicing.

If you find you are getting wild, return to practicing with your eyes open. Keep mixing up the two. Eyes open, eyes closed.

If you do this exercise fifteen minutes a day, within two weeks you will be pitching those balls in "blindly" with ease. You can then move back if you'd like to increase the difficulty.

How good you become simply depends on how much serious practice you are willing to do.

You can of course do the same thing with other objects so long as you are careful and don't attempt anything foolish or dangerous. I myself practice this little exercise with a dart board and darts. But I must point out that I always do my exercise completely alone. I would never risk injury to myself or another person. I caution you to heed the same advice.

This is wonderful exercise and a great confidence boost, but don't take it as a license to behave recklessly. Please, safety first, no arrows, no guns.

CHAPTER 8

EXERCISING YOUR MEMORY SYSTEMS

Memory, it goes without saying, is a major brain system so it's important to understand more or less what "remember" is all about (no, it's not an old song title.)

First of all, what exactly is a memory? Brainwise, it's what we're made of. It's our basic unit of being. In a very real sense, we are what we remember.

> *"Without memory we vanish, we cease to exist, our past is wiped out and yet we pay little attention to it except when it fails us. We do precious little to exercise it, to nurture it, to build it up, to protect it."*
> *—Mark Twain*

Memory records what we discover, learn, experience, feel. It records what we believe, expect, and, perhaps most importantly of all, it allows us to perceive that bizarre and inexplicable thing we call time.

In short, if memory is not the whole ball of wax, it sure is a large gooey part of it.

So, let's talk about how we actually use our memory in everyday life and what we can do to keep the neural nets that control our memory in top working order.

To start with, we actually employ three basic types of memories, each one handled by a different, but interconnected brain system.

The three types of memory can be described as fact memory, event memory, and skill memory. We'll take them in that order.

Fact Memory

Fact memory deals simply with information or facts, which is what most people think of when you say the word memorize. It's the system that handles stuff like your name, your rank, and your phone number plus the names of all your friends, all the animals, flowers, movie stars, and other stuff that you need to know in order to have a life. (Yes, it includes the facts of life as well).

Okay, this seems pretty straightforward but actually it's a little more complicated because fact memories are not just words, but also images, sounds, smells, touch, and even emotional feelings in various combinations all associated with some basic object or concept.

For example, the word "cat" summons up (in most people) an image of a furry little creature with a long tail. But it also summons up a whole lot of other stuff like the sound of purring and meowing, the tactile sensation of having something brush up against your leg, or maybe even the smell of cat food or cat doo-doo if you ever forgot to clean a litter box.

What I'm trying to get to here is that the memory "cat" can be triggered by any one of a number of different senses or combinations, some of which may not seem immediately obvious.

For example, you are in a fancy restaurant and suddenly you find yourself thinking "cat." A split second later you realize that you have just caught a faint whiff of something that smelled a lot like cat food. The memory came suddenly and unexpectedly because the trigger was not anticipated. (In this example, it's also a reason to suddenly recall the phrase "Check, please!")

Okay, so when we go to work on this system, one of the things we will stress is the interrelated memory triggers.

If you read a book or take a course in memory improvement (and almost always they are based only on fact memory), in a nutshell you will be taught various ways to strengthen the interconnections between the memory triggers. Save your money. The Tips and Techniques section in this chapter will reveal all you need to know.

Event Memory

Now this is the one we all like the most. This is remembering what happened to us in the past—the good times, the bad times, and, yes, even the boring times.

Event or experiential memory, as it is sometimes called, is of two basic flavors, short-term event memory (basically the last couple of weeks) and long-term event memory (the stuff way back there, like childhood memories).

The two systems are, of course, intimately connected because you can't have a long-term memory without first having a short-term one. Ah, you knew that, right?

The interesting question here is how does the old brain decide what to put into the long-term memory banks and what to toss out with last week's sports results?

"In the practical use of our intellect, forgetting is as important as remembering."—William James

Well, nobody knows for sure, but some researches think that we never really forget anything that happens to us. They believe it's all in there somewhere just waiting for a chance to come back up into consciousness.

Personally, I'm not so sure we remember absolutely everything, but I do believe we remember far more than we think we do.

We've all had that wonderful experience at one time or another of suddenly remembering something long forgotten. We know there's interesting stuff back in there somewhere. But the question is, how do we get it out?

Well, you could try a good hypnotist, but I have some simple exercises that will work just as well, if not better, and you won't have to worry about an embarrassing post-hypnotic suggestion.

The event exercises that follow will improve both short- and long-term memory.

I don't know about you, but when I have a really good time, I want to be able to savor every detail for years to come.

Skill Memory

Walk across a room, pick up the phone, dial it, wait for someone to answer, and begin speaking. Sounds like nothing. But these things take skill to do. Ask any four-year-old.

Skill memory is the ability to do the things we do every day, most of which we take for granted—like walking, for example. But if we injure a leg or foot or, God forbid, suffer a stroke, we suddenly realize just how much skill it takes to walk across a room.

Now just to make the distinction, life-support stuff (like breathing) is not a skill memory. That's part of the automatic system, the instinctive background system that luckily we all have. It makes our heart pump, tells us when we need food, when we need to drink water, and all that stuff.

Okay, so virtually everything else is a skill. Everything we consciously do, at one time or other we had to learn to do. And in the process, we had to lay down some memory tracks in order to be able to repeat it.

This skill-memory system is what allowed us to physically develop from children and adolescents into fully functioning adults.

And it wasn't easy, either. Remember that "awkward age"? When you had two left feet and your hands seemed to knock more stuff over than they were able to grab?

"A man's real possession is his memory.
In nothing else is he rich, in nothing else is he poor."
—Alexander Smith

But we overcame the obstacles and finally learned how to control our gangly extremities, at least most of us did. And as our skill memory became stronger and our basic motor skills became smoother and more automatic, we stopped thinking about most of what we were doing. It became a learned skill requiring no further mental effort. Okay, so what's the problem?

Well, for one thing, new skills are something we continue to learn throughout life. For another, skills not practiced will eventually be lost. The brain doesn't like to store a bunch of routines that we aren't using. Skill-memory space is apparently too precious to waste.

If we don't continue to do those things we so painfully and slowly learned, we will forget how to do them. Skill memory must be maintained. Yes, even simple stuff like walking and picking things up.

Fortunately, most of us keep up those basic skills without even thinking about it. But don't make the mistake of taking basic skills for granted. We all know what happens to the muscles of our bodies when we don't use them for long periods of time. Just remember, if you need to get back into shape physically, it all starts up top. Strong mind, strong body.

I have devised some simple tune-up exercises to keep the skill-memory circuits humming. Also, remember that all forms of physical exercise when done with concentration are in fact skill-memory exercises.

So when you do something physical like exercise or play a sport, think about what you are doing, concentrate on doing it better, and you will be exercising your brain as well as your body.

Not surprisingly, sports that involve exacting motor skills are best, but even simple stuff like running or walking, if you concentrate on form, gets the old brain involved in a positive way.

If you're not the athletic type, don't worry. There are plenty of skill exercises that don't involve the consumption of large quantities of calories.

Skill is not brute force anyway, it's deftness, touch. Building a house of cards takes as much a skill as hitting a baseball, throwing a dart, or executing a complex dance step. You may quibble about the relative level of difficulty, but all of these things are skills and all qualify as brain exercises.

The Exercises

EXERCISE

1

Fact-Memory Exercise

Obviously, memorizing lists or names and dates or even the phone book qualifies as fact-memory exercise. In fact, for the average brain, it's nearly impossible to get through a day without doing some sort of fact-memory work.

For one thing, you need to keep a kind of running memory of what time it is just so you won't miss your coffee breaks. Yes, clock watching can be a form of fact-memory exercise. But let's do something just a little more advanced.

Beginner

Here's an easy but good exercise. All of us, consciously or unconsciously, plan our day. Some of us are listmakers, some of us keep it simple and just think—I go to work, then I come home. End of plan.

Okay, starting tomorrow, become a listmaker. The list does not have to be long or even complete, but it needs to exist and it needs to have a minimum of six items on it. What sort of stuff? What you're going to do today, appointments, tasks, recreation. Putting down "Go to work" is fine; putting down "Go to lunch" is fine. Putting down "Mow the lawn" is fine.

But write at least six events down. And write things that actually will happen. This is not a wish list, this is an exercise.

Now estimate the time of day that each event will occur and write it down beside each entry.

Okay, that's it. Now, read over the list once and put it in your pocket. During the course of your day, mentally check off each item as it happens and at the same time try to remember the exact time you wrote down for it to occur. It doesn't matter if your estimation was correct or not, only that you remember what it was.

No cheating, do not refer to the original card, but do write down your recollections on a new card.

Okay, at the end of the day or the next morning if you like, check your cards to make sure they match. I know this sounds simple, but it is powerful.

Okay, now each day for at least two weeks, increase the complexity of your list by one item.

Intermediate

Rote memory exercise. Okay, this is the one that nobody likes, but believe me, it has great merit and recently has found renewed favor with educators. Yes, learning your multiplication tables and memorizing dates and little poems was good for you. So let's get back to it.

Tips & Techniques:

Before we go on, here are some of the promised tips about how to improve your performance on fact memory.

First of all, it helps to understand what's actually going on here. What we are trying to do when we commit information to memory is hand off, or transfer, some piece of information from our short-term memory into our long-term memory banks.

The problem is that the long-term memory system is very selective about what it will take in. It only likes to store information that it finds absolutely necessary or uniquely interesting. (That's why we can easily remember things that fascinate or amaze us).

So when we try to memorize something that we aren't all that excited about, the job becomes one of convincing our brain that the information is actually necessary to know. (Unfortunately, our memory manager doesn't find anxiety, panic, or even threats grounds for speeding up the review process.)

In order to get something by the gate keeper up there, we have to use the information again and again. Basically, we have to prove to our long-term memory manager that we really are going to use this information often. We constantly resubmit the data storage request until finally it's approved and the information is filed away. (Sounds very similar to the way government bureaucracy works, doesn't it?)

Anyway, that's what the repetition is all about. Do it over and over. It is, hands down, the best way to commit something to long-term memory. But for those of you who just have to have a shortcut, yes, there are a few tricks that can be used to sneak in the back door.

Luckily, human memory is an interconnected system, which as we have learned can be triggered by more than one type of sensory input. The trick is to connect something you want to remember with one or more triggers that are easier for you to remember.

For example, if you visualize well (see the exercises on pages 94–107 if you don't) then you would probably take your list from the beginner exercise, look at it, and form a picture in your mind of how the written words look. When you remember "Lunch, 12:05" you would not be recalling the abstract number 12:05, but rather the image of it written down. Simple enough.

Okay, so what else can you do if you don't have a great visual memory? Well, there is the actual writing-experience memory (sometimes incorrectly called muscle memory). Most of us get a memory boost by the act of writing something down. Why? Because we now have a skill memory linked with a

(continued on page 116)

fact memory. Notice how people who have trouble remembering how to spell a word will write the word out to see how it looks. The act of writing triggers the memory. The reason is the extra link, the association if you prefer big technical words.

What you're actually doing is taking a side door into the room where the memory is stored. All memories have side doors, usually lots of them. The trick is to find the door that's easiest to get into, the one that doesn't have a slippery doorknob.

Okay, you say this approach doesn't help you at all. Every time you write something down, you instantly forget it. Why? Because the reason you wrote it down was so that you wouldn't have to remember it. Duh.

But, if you maintain a consciousness of the act of writing something down, watch yourself form the words or characters, and repeat the associated sounds out loud as you do it, you will make a much stronger connection and your ability will improve. Also try to form a mental picture of the words or characters after you've written them down. Close your eyes for a moment and form an image of what you have just written. The more attention you pay to what you are doing and the more ways you think about it, the stronger the memory will be.

Here's another tip that may seem counter-intuitive at first. Remembering the familiar is far more difficult than remembering the strange.

We have already talked about the brain needing new, fresh, non-routine input to be challenged. Something out of the ordinary piques the brain's interest and sharpens the senses.

Well, guess what? The memory circuits work the same way. Bizarre or unusual information is always the easiest to remember. That's why we vividly remember the time the boss tripped and spilled coffee all over his new suit or, more somberly, where we were when the Challenger exploded.

So how do we put this to work? Simple. If you need to remember something, package the information in an unusual way. Write it down in red ink or, better yet, on a piece of red paper, or on something that you normally wouldn't write on, say, a banana. Believe me, and I speak from experience, anything you write down on a banana you are not going to easily forget.

Okay, suppose, "Yes, you have no bananas," what then? Well, if you have only black ink and conventional paper, try writing it down backwards or top to bottom, diagonals are nice too. Something strange and unusual. The more exotic, the better.

You get the idea, make the experience of remembering memorable.

(continued on page 117)

All right, one more. The "How to Improve Your Memory" books love this one. It's called substitution. What you do is associate some fact or piece of information with something unrelated. For example, you need to remember that you have a four twenty-five appointment on Thursday. So you associate the time with let's say apples. Four hours are four apples; twenty-five minutes are twenty-five seeds.

Now you've got to remember Thursday. What happened on Thursday that you find memorable? You got married, your team won the pennant, or how about just, it rained last Thursday?

Rain, four apples, twenty-five apple seeds. You say that to yourself a couple of times. Two days later, trust me, all you have to think is rain and apples, and the numbers and dates will come.

Now I've always thought systems like this were a little elaborate, but they do work. For people who absolutely must commit stuff to memory on a regular basis and have trouble, these kinds of oddball associations can help a lot.

You can also do pictograph substitutions. Draw a little picture, say, of a sunflower with only two petals. The petals point to a clock time. For that matter, just draw a clock face. The combination of drawing it, along with the visual image, will help you remember it without ever looking at it again. All you have to do is remember drawing it and mentally look at what you drew. Amazing, but true.

So what have we learned? Make it strange or associate it, and you won't forget. Of course, practice doesn't hurt either. The very best way to improve your memory is to use it as often as possible.

All right, you hate the idea of memorizing. But I'm not asking you to memorize the Gettysburg address or even the phone book. Well, actually I am going to ask you to memorize the phone book, but a small one, your own.

You probably know most of the numbers of your good friends, or did before speed dialing became ubiquitous. So, now learn the rest.

Take one number a day. (If you don't like your friends, use your rolodex at work and do business associates.) Just memorize it. A good way to solidify it is to tap it into a dialing pad as you say it silently to yourself. But whatever, commit the numbers and name to memory.

Okay, work on it once in the morning, then a couple of more times during the day. Keep at it till you've got it. If you find one number a day too daunting, then do one every two days, or even one a week. Volume is unimportant, it is purely the doing that counts. Remember, we are exercising the brain. Remembering phone numbers is only a byproduct, a side benefit. Hopefully, a useful one.

Okay, so you already know everybody's phone number or ten digits is too heavy for you. Then do birthdays. Or if phone numbers are too easy, do addresses and include zip codes. Stop at social security numbers however, or your friends might think you are moonlighting with the IRS.

Okay, if you don't like the idea of personal information, other things you can memorize on a daily or weekly basis include lines of poetry or fiction (yes, the Gettysburg address is a good one), lines from the Bible (I'm a King James fan myself), or the Talmud or Koran or other spiritual source, depending on what works for you.

Lighter stuff? How about song lyrics? Memorize one full song per week for six weeks. This one is usually pretty easy because of the musical cues. See what I mean about associative triggers?

Then, of course, there is stuff like Haiku for you esoteric types and good old limericks for the earthy. One a week is plenty. Be sure to impress your friends by reciting them on every possible occasion.

Fact: Research into memory techniques used by ordinary people indicates that we tend to use one of two basic approaches when faced with the task of rote memorization of words.

Either we picture the information in our mind's eye and try to visually remember it or we silently repeat the information over and over to ourselves.

Is one method better than the other?

While both methods are effective, the studies indicate that the success rate is higher in those individuals who repeat the information over and over to themselves.

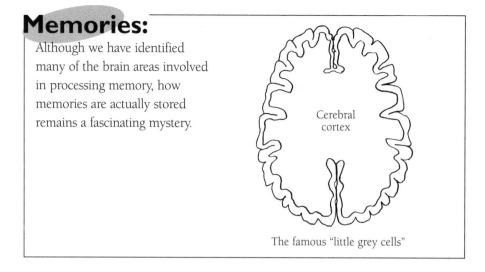

Memories:

Although we have identified many of the brain areas involved in processing memory, how memories are actually stored remains a fascinating mystery.

Cerebral cortex

The famous "little grey cells"

Last chance for those who hate literature, music, and have no friends. *TV Guide*. Memorize the evening listings two days in advance of the broadcasts. Do this every day for at least two weeks.

Advanced

Remember that thing called a library? Head on down there and look for the poetry section. (Yes, poetry, and for your information it's coming back in a big way. In fact, the major cities are all sporting "poetry cafes" again where new poets read their latest efforts in competitions dubbed "slams.")

Okay, go through the racks. Pull out books and browse until you find something that stirs you and gives you a strong reaction—like "Wow, that's really lovely" or "too true, too true."

Pick out a poem, a good-sized one, at least sonnet-length, more if you can handle it. Now memorize it.

Work on it as often as you can. Take your time, make this a full six-week project if you like. The goal is to be able to recite the whole thing from memory.

You don't have do this publicly if you are shy, but you should practice it out loud as the vocalization adds a strong cue. Phrasing and emotional delivery also help set down

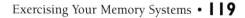

Fact: Reciting from memory is impressive, mainly because it's so rare these days. But not too long ago it was common to be able to recite a favorite verse or two from memory (and very useful when it came to the ritual of courting).

And before literacy became widespread, fact memory was actually a necessity, a survival skill. Thousands of years of human history, science, and literature were handed down orally long before someone figured out how to notate it on stone or clay tablets, let alone invent paper and ink.

Just consider this one prodigious feat of human memory as an example of what we are capable of.

The Iliad and *The Odyssey*, both novel-length stories, made a journey of over six hundred years from storyteller to storyteller, before finally being written down by the ancient Greeks.

(Homer didn't know how to operate a quill pen, much less a laptop.)

the memory tracks, so feel free to interpret. Remember you are not the character Data on "Star Trek." You're human, you have emotions; use them. Tie them into the work to strengthen the connection. Remember nobody is listening, unless of course you choose to let someone listen. Believe me, if you get the whole thing down and can bring yourself to recite it for someone, you'll be a hit.

Another option for the socially advanced student. Join a local theatre or a University theatre and take a part in a play. Not only will you have to learn your lines by heart, but you will also have to memorize physical movements, a definite plus.

If, sadly, you have no local amateur theatre or are unable to win a part, another option is to form your own group and do your own reading or staged reading "off book," as they say in the theatre. That is, everybody learns their part and delivers it on cue while sitting down comfortably in someone's living room (refreshments are optional, but strongly advised). It's good exercise and, also, lots of fun.

EXERCISE

Event Memory Exercise

► We will break this down into two exercises. One for short-term and one for long-term event memory.

Beginner

Short Term—Pick an event in your life that has occurred in the recent past, at least a week old, not older than two weeks. By event I mean something that happened to or around you. It could be an interaction such as a conversation (witnessed or participatory), a movie or television show you saw, a visit to a doctor's office, or perhaps a task you undertook like cleaning out a closet or some job you did at work. The event should not be terribly long, but reasonably vivid.

Okay, sit in a comfortable chair. You may close your eyes or leave them open, but you should not focus on anything too interesting. Likewise, do not allow any noise or other stimulation to intrude during this exercise. In plain English, find a nice quiet spot, one you are comfortable in and like. Think back and remember the event. Start from the beginning and go through it to the end. Move through it, if possible. Remember

Short-term:

The brain structure that mediates our consciousness is the hippocampus. It may also control short term memory.

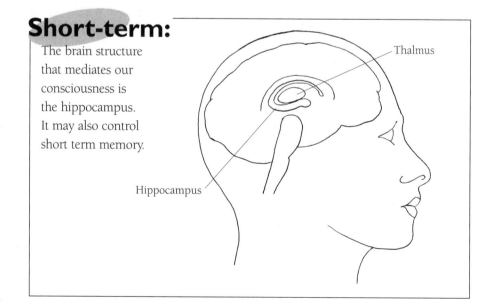

Thalmus

Hippocampus

everything that you can. Try as best as you can to re-experience it. Don't worry if at first you don't remember everything, or even all that much, just start. Go through the event several times. Try to fill in the details—add conversations if there were any; sounds, smells, visuals, any and everything you can remember. If you like, pretend you are being interrogated by a friendly policeman. Imagine you are a vital witness and must remember exactly what happened. Speak out loud if you find it helpful. Do this for no more than fifteen minutes. An hour or two later, come back and do it again. See if you remember more. Try remembering the same event in the same way for several days in a row until you are quite sure you have milked it for all you can remember. The next week, pick a new event and repeat the exercise. Do this for six weeks.

Not only will you find your event memory getting sharper, but you will become more perceptive about what is going on around you, what you are experiencing. You'll find yourself beginning to think like a trained observer. That's a brain skill that you will find carries over into many other areas.

(A version of this exercise is used by professional fiction writers to sharpen their descriptive skills. You'll find it, along with some other interesting exercises in chapter 12, titled "How the Pros Exercise Their Brains.")

Long Term—Okay, this is very similar to the short-term exercise except that we are only going to use one event. This should be something from at least five or ten years ago. It can even be an event from childhood. Pick a memory that is important to you—a special celebration or holiday that you remember, a graduation, a wedding you attended or were in, or even a vacation. This event can be one that took place over several days or weeks if you like and should be something

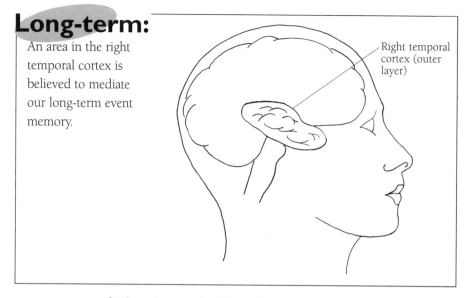

Long-term:

An area in the right temporal cortex is believed to mediate our long-term event memory.

Right temporal cortex (outer layer)

fairly substantial. The only restriction is that it be a fond memory. This isn't therapy, it's exercise. No angst, please.

Find the comfortable place and relive it. Remember as much as you can. Spend no more than half an hour at a time, but work on the same memory for a least a month, milk everything you can out of it. Pretend you are planning your memoirs. A publisher is talking six figures, the ghost writer has just turned on his tape recorder, so make sure you give him as much detail as possible.

By the way, both the short- and long-term memory exercises can be done while traveling. In fact, if you commute to work by public transportation and forgot to pick up something to read, it's a great way to spend the time.

Intermediate and Advanced

For the intermediate and advanced versions of these exercises, write down your recollection in the form of a factual report. Concentrate less on the amount of detail as on the relevance. Think of yourself as a reporter for a newspaper. What was important about what happened in this event? How much does the reader really want to know?

Another approach is to view the event as a short story. In this case you may embellish the memories as long as you recognize that you are doing so. You can put in how you feel and your intuitive memories about what you think may have been going on. If you try this one, you will be well on your way to understanding where fiction comes from and how it is created.

Skill-Memory Exercise

Beginning level exercises involve reorientation and maintenance of existing skills, as well as reintroducing skills we once possessed but—for one reason or another—have abandoned.

To start with, here are a few simple things you can do with common daily skills.

1. If you drive a car, particularly if you drive to work on a regular basis, this is a good opportunity to exercise a skill you undoubtedly take for granted, driving. (If you don't drive, don't bother reading this, just skip ahead to the next exercise.)

Okay, in order to turn your boring daily commute into a skill-improvement exercise, do the following.

From the time you first enter the car, maintain a conscious awareness of what you are about to do. If you like playing games, pretend you are back in high school and you have just gotten your driver's license. This is your first day behind the wheel by yourself. (By the way, if you can remember the actual experience you can be doing a long-term event-memory exercise simultaneously.)

Now, the focus of your task will be to execute your drive as perfectly as possible from a technique point of view. As soon as you get in the car do a safety check, make sure the car is out of gear and the brake is set. Adjust your seat and all mirrors if necessary, make sure you're buckled in. Now start the engine. Let it warm up properly while you check all of the gauges.

As you engage and begin to drive, pretend you have a delicate object balanced in the seat next to you, a three-tiered cake you are delivering to a wedding. Accelerate smoothly and evenly. When you brake, do so smoothly, so you don't upset the cake. Be precise about your turns. Try to make them letter perfect and also keep your speed as constant as possible.

Obey all laws to the letter. By the way, traffic tickets are definitely not part of brain exercise.

Drive with an awareness of what's around you. Anticipate the need to slow down or stop and try to deaccelerate, as much as safety permits, by easing off the accelerator rather than making heavy use of the brakes. (This is how you are supposed to drive, assuming you care about such things as fuel efficiency and saving money.)

You can also do this little exercise on a run to the store. You don't need to do it every day, more like once a week. It's a sharpening exercise. The idea is to remember that driving a car is a skill, one that you know but one you need to occasionally reaffirm. By the way, if you find you had a little trouble driving absolutely smoothly, then you probably should continue to treat every drive as an exercise until you can do so.

2. Longhand writing is another common skill we all possess and we all take for granted. I, for one, find myself so attuned to using a keyboard that when I am called upon to actually write something out by hand, I find it sometimes feels like I'm writing with a lead weight attached to my hand. My fluidity is gone because I no longer write longhand on a daily basis. If this is also the case for you, do some writing exercise every day. (As I now do.)

When writing as an exercise, concentrate on penmanship more than content. One easy way to do this is to simply practice your signature (something that with many busy people degenerates into a frightening scrawl).

You can also copy a phrase or sentence over ten or fifteen times in a row. If you find that boring, write a letter to someone and copy it out a second time making it as neat and pretty as possible. (No, you don't have to send the letter. It's an exercise.) Do this once a day for at least six weeks.

3. A Couple of Simple Ones.

Get out a deck of cards and shuffle it for five minutes. Concentrate on smoothness and evenness. If you like, deal out imaginary hands.

Take a twenty-minute walk in which you concentrate on maintaining a correct posture and a precise stride. Same can be done as a fast walk, jog, or run. But remember to concentrate on form.

When you do any regular task such as make dinner, open the mail, mow the lawn, clean the house, do the laundry, make yourself aware of your exact movements as you execute them. Try to make each movement precise and efficient. Anticipate what you are going to do next and think about ways to improve your physical performance. Make yourself more efficient. If it is safe to do so (no knives or sharp objects, please), increase your speed. In short, try to do it better.

On the subject of skills that have waned, you are going to have to do a little event-memory work first. For example, did you ever play a musical instrument? At some time in your youth did you become proficient at some recreational skill like playing jacks, throwing darts, playing ping pong, shooting baskets, or something artistic like drawing or painting? Maybe you knitted or did beadwork or put models together.

Anything that was once one of your skills, but you have let slide will work.

Reintroduce yourself to whatever it was. Do it again. See how good or bad you are at it now. The bonus here is that you should trigger some event memories. You will also be doing some brain-invigoration exercises if it was something you once enjoyed doing. Chances are it was.

Intermediate and Advanced

The next level would be to engage in some regular skill exercise with the idea of constantly improving yourself.

Examples of this include virtually all forms of sports. Simply find one that you enjoy, are capable of doing to a reasonable level, and can find time to engage in. Remember, there are skills for everyone regardless of physique or even conditioning. For example, you need very little strength to throw English-style darts or to play pool or billiards.

By the way, group sports like softball, volleyball, or bowling are excellent choices for brains that have trouble with initiation—the social interaction increases motivation.

If you do not have a competitive or sporting nature, then consider taking up a craft such as model making, pottery or clay modeling, carpentry, sewing, or even just building houses made of playing cards.

Then there are the artistic skills such as playing a musical instrument, singing, dancing, drawing, or painting.

Even simple doodling is a skill exercise as long as you do it regularly

Fact: Skill patterns can become addictive just like drugs. Psychologists call it "addictive behavior." You've probably heard the term work-a-holic, but you can also be a sports-a-holic, a computer game-a-holic, even a dance-a-holic.

Although physiologists might categorize such behavior as "abnormal," society often rewards it. Skill-addicted people are frequently overachievers.

The line between human dedication and human obsession is a fine one. Don't expect me to draw it for you.

and endeavor to improve by increasing the exactness or complexity of your doodles.

Some computer games, the ones with paddles and hand–eye coordination stuff in them, are okay, too (as long as you remember to have a life).

CHAPTER 9

DAYDREAMING: THE KEY TO SUCCESS

How to Exercise Your Imagination Through Daydreaming and in the Process Open up Your Career Possibilities

Kids have a natural tendency to daydream, especially during a tedious Latin class or some other equally boring event, which they are forced by adults to attend.

If you ask an eight-year-old to sit still in a chair for say ten minutes (assuming you have such amazing powers of persuasion), within about three minutes you will see the eyes start to gaze into the distance as he or she retreats into that magical netherworld that we call daydreaming.

It's a wonderful mental ability kids have that we adults also share but too often shun. Unfortunately, as we grow taller, we also grow more skeptical of the power of daydreaming, believing it to be, in adults, the profession of idlers and dreamers.

In reality, the opposite is true. Daydreaming is a tool of the doer.

"The possible's slow fuse is lit by the imagination."
—Emily Dickenson

So what is daydreaming, anyway? Well, very much the opposite of night dreaming for a start.

Let's compare them. Night dreams tend to be passive. Something seemingly very real happens to us over which we have little or no control. We are at the mercy of the unfolding events and the outcome is uncertain. Night dreams are usually surprising, bizarre, and annoyingly incomplete.

We often wake up puzzled by our night dreams. We tell our friends about the strange events, ask their opinion, we might even seek professional advice as to the meaning, if any.

Sometimes the imagined events spin terribly out of control and we wake up suddenly in a cold sweat, a nightmare.

But daydreams work differently. The events in them tend to be directed by our consciousness or at least by our semiconscious mind. We actively do something or become something in our daydreams, something we want to do or want to be.

We generally choose the subject matter or at least have script approval and we control the flow of events as we are imagining them.

As a result, daydreams rarely, if ever, spin out of our control and are generally pleasurable experiences, which is why our teachers kept telling us when we were children to wake up and pay attention.

They assumed, rightly, that we purposely daydreamed to escape their dreary class and to have fun which, of course, was not the point of school.

So does daydreaming have a useful purpose other than relief from boredom? Of course it does.

It's an imagination exercise designed to help us develop our self-image when we are young by role-playing. It also helps us set and plan our goals, and strengthens our desire to carry through our plans by tantalizing us with the imagined rewards of our efforts.

In short, it's a first-class, all-around motivation exercise. Ask any very successful person and they will tell you that they first daydreamed of their success as kids.

Okay, that's great for children, but what about us poor brain-dead adults?

For adults, it's an even more valuable exercise. Why? Because as an adult you can focus the imagination much more precisely. And because of your greater experience, you can more easily gauge the gap between the fantasy of imagination and the reality that you want to obtain.

You see, when you're a child, the line between fantasy and reality is very blurry and uncertain. It sharpens as you get older which makes dealing with the world a little easier. But take care, the line should never become completely fixed or your possibilities will become fixed as well.

In fact, very creative people draw the line as faintly as possible, knowing that the boundary can too easily become a wall.

"Yes, I am a dreamer. For a dreamer is one who only finds his way by moonlight, and his punishment is that he sees the dawn before the rest of the world."—Oscar Wilde

Unfortunately, many adults cut themselves off from their imagination, wrongly believing it to be an impediment to logical, sensible behavior. They view daydreaming as a child's toy, no longer of any use except maybe to some weird artist. The result is they deprive themselves of an extremely valuable and powerful mental tool.

But the good news is that imagination can always be revived and restored, even after years of neglect. So stop using your daydreaming circuits just to escape from a long-forgotten history class, and put them to good use the way they were intended.

The exercise outline below will show you how to put day-dreaming to use as a career-improvement motivator. It's a method with which most highly successful people are already familiar. We will see variations of this exercise in Chapter 12 on professional exercises. Here we start with the basic approach.

EXERCISE

1

The Stuff That Dreams Are Made of

Please note that this exercise has no beginner or intermediate level. There is only one way to do this, advanced. This exercise is for those who want to make a real difference in the quality of how they live their lives.

For your first session of this exercise, you should be alone and in a comfortable and safe place. The surroundings must be as pleasant as possible. An easy chair by a window is one example, assuming the view is a peaceful or happy one. You could also sit by a fire if you like staring at the flames, or you could lie down on a couch, on your bed, or even do this exercise in a bubble bath. Whatever makes you comfortable is the key.

It should be a relatively quiet place, however playing music in the background is okay as long as it is only instrumental music. No singing. Lyrics are too distracting.

Food and drink is fine. If you're a smoker now is not the time to quit. But no alcohol or other serious mood-altering drugs, please.

The idea here is calm, safe, happy, but also alert. This is not nap time.

Now do your dead level best to put all worries and thoughts about what you have to do tomorrow or who you are mad at out of your head. It's also not the time to criticize

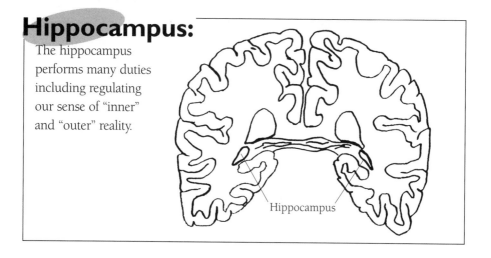

Hippocampus:

The hippocampus performs many duties including regulating our sense of "inner" and "outer" reality.

Hippocampus

yourself for some recent lapse or gaff. Think positive thoughts about yourself only. For now, you have no faults. You're a peach of a human being.

By the way, in order to clear your head it sometimes helps to think briefly about an upcoming event that you are looking forward to, or back to a pleasant event you have recently experienced. Think to yourself that you would like to have those experiences more often and that soon you will be able to.

Okay, now down to work. Outline in your head your particular goal for this year.

Suppose you want to move up in the company, become a manager. Or suppose you want to close a big deal or meet a sales projection. Suppose you want to strike out on your own and start a business or consulting firm. Or let's say your goal is to improve your performance at some task you already perform. Maybe you just want to be more successful socially or in school. Whatever your goal is, outline it in your head.

Envision it concretely as a state of being to be obtained.

Now, imagine yourself having already obtained the goal. Slam dunk, you're magically there! Start dreaming about it. Imagine exactly how it will feel. Let your mind explore all the new benefits you will enjoy. See them, feel them, taste them. Use that imagination of yours to daydream your goal into a very real imagined reality.

Since this is your first session, you are allowed to let your fantasy go wild. Imagine the best possible results, no downside, it all happens just the way you want it to happen.

Let yourself enjoy this fantasy for at least fifteen minutes but no longer than thirty.

"The problems of the world cannot possibly be solved by skeptics or cynics whose horizons are limited by the obvious realities. We need men [and women] who can dream of things that never were."
—John F. Kennedy

Now pull yourself back into the present, but don't lose the glow. Move from your safe place back into some limited contact with the real world. Take a walk outside, if possible. You can walk alone, in a park or the woods, or down a street with people on it, but try not to run into anyone you will have to talk to as this will break your concentration. Yes, you are still exercising.

Okay, now begin to examine the differences between the reality you imagined and the one that you are now in. Tell yourself that the two are not really very far apart. List the differences if you like. Now imagine again that you are that future person walking down the street. Your goal has been obtained. The world is the same, but you have changed your relationship to it. Fix on this feeling in all it's positive aspects.

You may continue your walk for up to one hour. During this time you will have been working to convince yourself that your goals are very reasonable, very obtainable, and that, most importantly, you will get there.

End your session by some social contact or pre-planned event if possible. Do not discuss your dream with anyone. You may, however, disclose your future plans, but do not discuss your future vision of yourself, rather try to project it. Be that person. Display the quiet confidence of a successful person and feel, believe, and finally know, that you will get there.

Okay, that's only the first session. Future sessions can be shorter and can take place in other settings if you like. But, after the initial session, begin to direct your daydream.

What you want to begin to do now is to trace your path back to the goal. Yes, look at it in retrospect. Remember the steps you took to get there, the steps you have in reality not yet taken. Think them through and see yourself doing them. Remember, in your daydream, they are already done.

End each session with a careful return to the real world and a careful examination of how much space remains between your future goal and the actual reality that you do live in. Your task here is to convince your brain that the dream and reality are on an inevitable collision course.

Gradually, maybe even quickly, the distance will shrink. You will fill yourself with such confidence and drive that the real world will have no choice but to merge with your vision of it.

Remember, it is a proven fact that our belief in ourselves strongly affects what actually happens to us. The circuitry is there in all of us to control it. And all we've got to do is a little brain exercise!

By the way, a note for the skeptics who would point out that all our dreams can't become a complete reality: While that may be true, those who have both won and lost will tell you that even if a goal is never met, it's better to have lived believing it was going to happen than not.

After all, enjoying the daily glow of confidence beats the hell out of wallowing in miserable resignation.

A Planned Escape Is Best

The most common use of the daydream, some would say, unfortunately, is escapism. But there are times in life and situations where this brain function is very necessary and very protecting.

We've all had to do things we don't want to do in life and sometimes for a very long period of time. In these cases, judicial use of daydreaming to escape from drudgery or outright misery is a very good thing.

It can even work in a similar way to the previous exercise, by lifting us out of a situation over which we have no control and saying to our brains that one day we will be out of here.

A friend of mine once found himself—for reasons that need not be illuminated—mired in heavy debt. For some years he was forced to maintain a job he virtually hated in order to pay off the debt.

Naturally, you would expect a person in such a position to look pretty hangdog, or at least to complain regularly of the misery he was enduring.

And yet whenever I met him on the street he was always amazingly cheerful, in fact, downright positive. This behavior piqued my curiosity and caused me to inquire after the secret to his very healthy attitude.

I speculated that maybe he had become a Buddhist or had found some terrific girlfriend that made it all worthwhile. Neither turned out to be the case.

He admitted to me that he had a secret vice.

Once a week, he bought a lottery ticket. He explained that he always bought the ticket six days in advance of the lottery, never at the last minute and that he never bought more than one.

Knowing he was a logical, level-headed fellow who understood that the odds to the lottery were millions to one against him, I asked how this in any way could help? After all, he couldn't realistically expect to actually win.

Ah, he said, but that was the key. As long as he held that ticket in his wallet, he was able to convince himself that he was already a millionaire. He daydreamed throughout the week about how he would simply walk away from the job once his winning ticket was confirmed, without so much as looking back.

So every time he was reminded of the unpleasant reality he was living, his mind was able to block or lessen the sting by simply thinking, "Hey, come Saturday, I'm out of here."

He pointed out that by buying the ticket six days in advance, he need spend only one day a week in the absolute certainty of reality.

The very next day he bought a fresh ticket and for the price of one dollar a week was able to maintain his sanity and his cheerful demeanor.

He pointed out that it was a lot cheaper than either a bar tab or a psychiatrist and I had to agree with him!

I should point out that he never did win the lottery, but two years later, he did succeed in paying off the debt. He then quit the hated job and has now moved on to become highly successful in a completely different field, one of his own choosing. To my knowledge, he never bought another lottery ticket. He no longer needs to.

And by the way, he was also using the other daydream exercise all along to project himself into the future he now enjoys!

CHAPTER 10

BRAIN STRETCHES

How to Loosen up Your Brain and Keep It Hungry for New Ideas

Too often as we grow older we loose flexibility in our mental processes. Our thinking becomes a fixed pattern with little variation. Our brains grow rigid. We may even discover to our dismay that we have become that thing we always said we would never become, narrow-minded.

The scary thing is how quickly it can happen, sometimes before we're out of our twenties. I've even seen some teenagers showing signs. How does it happen?

Well, certainly not maliciously. We just fall into mental routines that are comfortable because they are easy and not very taxing. We find simple mental solutions that work for us, that make us feel comfortable, and basically get us through the day.

It's just plain old laziness. The same thing that turns our muscles into mush and gives us that unwanted extra body mass. The vast unused power of our brain becomes exactly like so much unused muscle, a flabby mess.

Unfortunately, we don't grow a midriff bulge around our cranium to alert us to the deteriorating state of our synaptic circuits. In fact, we probably believe our brain circuits are in fine shape, as good as they ever were.

Okay, so what about some moderate exercise? Some basic stretches to wake up those lazy synapses and maybe quicken the neural processing circuits? How about just a little brain jogging, nothing too serious?

All right, here are some exercises for you. They are designed to simply get you out of your rut, stretch out the way you think, and wake you up.

The Exercises

These exercises are not graded because they are simply designed to give the brain a jog and stretch it out.

How often or intensely you choose to do the exercises becomes the gradation. You can just loosen up by doing them or you could really get into it.

Rather like physical activity, you may find yourself enjoying the process of exercising more than you thought you would.

EXERCISE

1

Concerning That "Other" Hand

Most people not only favor one hand over the other, they pretty much use one hand exclusively. They relegate the "other," untrained hand to simple, low-coordination tasks like lifting and carrying. Very seldom does this poor neglected "other" hand get to do anything even remotely complicated.

A good way to stretch the brain is to find some of those long-dormant circuits and fire them up! We're going to start involving that "other" hand a little more, maybe even try to make it earn it's keep.

Okay, so how do we go about doing that?

One way is to start having what I call "alternative" days.

Once a week or so for an entire day, just decide that you will use your other hand for all tasks that it can possibly handle.

If you like, pretend that your favored hand is temporarily out of commission or maybe employ a little role reversal. Treat your favored hand like your "other" hand and vice versa.

However you do it, the goal is to use your favored hand as little as possible and your "other" hand as much as possible.

Now to be sensible, we have to make exceptions and call a time out for very complex tasks like writing and, of course, for situations where safety could be an issue. (I do not want you to try operating a vehicle, a power tool, or doing anything that could remotely be considered dangerous with your "other" hand. Period. I don't want you to get hurt or hurt anyone else, okay?)

But for all the simple picking up and moving around stuff, you can easily and safely use your "other" hand.

Start right out with breakfast. Try using a fork and a spoon with your "other" hand. Pick up your juice glass or coffee cup with your "other" hand. (Do be careful with all hot liquids. Don't try it if you feel you might drop it. Again, safety first!)

And when you leave the house, put the things you normally carry in your pockets on your "other" side only.

Just think of everything you do as reversed. It's a stretch, but then that's the point!

Here's a tip. When the tasks become a little more complicated, like opening and closing a change purse or small box, try to think what your favored hand would do and then get your "other" hand to duplicate the motion from its point of view.

You'll be surprised to find that your "other" hand can handle most small tasks that you do quite well.

Now you may make some clumsy mistakes here and there and maybe even find your other hand going off in entirely the wrong direction. This can be a little frustrating at first, but just stick with it. Pay attention and take it real slow.

Remember your "other" hand will not be able to match the speed of your favored hand. Quickness and skill come with practice.

Now if you find the idea of using your "other" hand for an entire day too overwhelming, try shorter periods, say an hour at a time. Come on, you can handle that!

Another interesting approach is time-sharing. Break your world down into hemispheres. Anything to the right, you pick up with your right hand. Anything to the left, use your left hand. Let your orientation be your guide. This is a good approach if you work in an office and sit at a desk all day.

Yet another interesting stretch is to teach your "other" hand a specific task. A good one is how to use a key.

Now this will take a fair amount of practice but if you stay with it, you'll find it's actually a useful skill. There are times when it's very convenient to be able to open a lock with your "other" hand.

Fact: We have all heard about those exotic individuals who are ambidextrous, that is to say able to use either hand for complicated tasks.

But did you know that very few of them are naturally ambidextrous?

It turns out most people who can use both hands with equal skill simply taught themselves how to do it.

They just decided that since God gave them two hands, they might as well use them both.

Start by simply letting your "other" hand carry your key chain on your way up to the door. Practice letting your "other" hand single out the key you need off the ring.

Next, try to actually get the key in the lock. Now I warn you, this is usually the toughest part to learn and it can be very frustrating. It's not a bad idea to start by letting your favored hand help out a little. Use it to guide your "other" hand, but be careful not to let it take over the job.

If you stick with it and practice, you will find that your other hand can eventually manipulate a lock with the same ease and skill as your favored hand.

You will have done a nice little piece of brain stretching and come up with a useful new skill in the bargain!

Child's Play

Children are always stretching out their brains, trying out different circuits, trying to look at the world in strange and funny ways. It's basically how they first discover and then develop their neural circuitry.

The sad thing is adults are always trying to get them to stop doing this. Although they resist for as long as they can, sooner or later the kids do finally succumb. They give up their natural exploration and accept a worldview that has been fashioned by long-held tradition.

"Young men's minds are always changeable, but when an old man is concerned in the matter, he looks both before and after."—Homer

Luckily a few don't give up quite so easily. They are usually the ones that push back the envelope and give us a new way of looking at the world. They remind us that reality is an infinite tapestry that can be approached in many different ways.

The reality we think we know is merely the view that we choose to accept. We have no way of knowing for sure if it is accurate. In fact, the only thing we do know for sure is that it is, at best, incomplete.

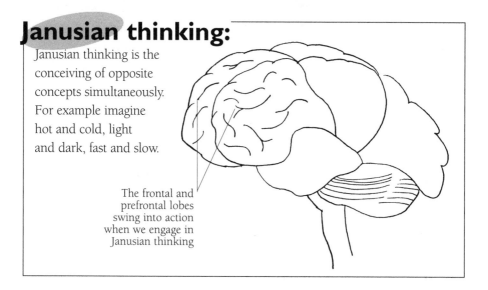

Janusian thinking:

Janusian thinking is the conceiving of opposite concepts simultaneously. For example imagine hot and cold, light and dark, fast and slow.

The frontal and prefrontal lobes swing into action when we engage in Janusian thinking

There is an infinity of alternative viewpoints and as long as there are children in the world, these alternative realities will thankfully continue to be explored.

Okay, so let's return for just a little while to one of those childhood realities and stretch our brains out. Let's explore a world that almost all children discover at some point, the upside-down world.

You probably did this as a child. I know I did. But I bet you haven't done it recently.

All you have to do for this brain stretch is find a nice comfy spot on the floor and lay down. You can use a pillow or mat if you like.

Lay on your back and look up at the ceiling. (A favorite place of mine to lay down was always half under the dining room table so I could see it looming in the foreground.)

Now the idea is simple. The world is upside down. Gravity is reversed.

Imagine yourself walking across the ceiling, stepping around the light fixtures and archways. Everything you see rising up is really hanging there, suspended in space. Try and figure out why stuff doesn't fall to the ceiling floor. Strange that some objects seem not to be anchored at all.

It's a interesting world. Feel free to change locations or to make a ninety-degree rotation. Walking on walls is fun, too.

A Foreign Tongue

One of the most fascinating abilities that human brains possess is language: The ability to put our thoughts into words and communicate those words to other brains who then translate them back into thoughts.

The only problem is that we seem to have very different ideas about how a given word should sound and look. Human brains speak hundreds of different languages and dialects.

Despite this fact, too many of us ignore the linguistic wealth and are content to live out our lives speaking and understanding only one single language.

Our brain can certainly handle more than one language. In fact, there are people who speak a dozen or more languages. And it's certainly not at all uncommon for people in border areas to speak at least two.

So popular has our own English language become that there are now many more people who speak it as a second language than native-born speakers.

So, if your brain is monolingual or mostly so, perhaps it's time to stretch out your synapses just a little and explore another way to describe the world and code your thoughts.

Now, if the very idea of learning a foreign language strikes terror in your heart, let me give you a little aid and encouragement.

First of all, there is a common myth that monolingual adults cannot successfully learn a new language. Not true.

You can learn a second language from scratch at any age. People do it all the time.

Okay, so let's say you're game. You want to give it a try. What's the best way to go about it?

Start by deciding whether or not your primary interest is in speaking a language or just being able to read and understand it. Remember you can be fluent and illiterate and the reverse is nearly true.

If you would like the wonderful social experience of speaking a different language then one of the best and most fun ways is the learning system known as the immersion method. This is where you are thrown into the new language and basically deprived of the one you normally use. It's a sink-or-swim proposition and it gets good, fast results. Many language schools offer "weekend immersion retreats" where you get a crash course and have a lot of fun, too. Try looking for such a program in your area.

If understanding the written word is more your cup of tea, then consult your local university or language institute about signing up for some basic grammar courses.

"We should make things as simple as possible, but not simpler."—Albert Einstein

Now, suppose like me, you had some language instruction in high school and maybe college. Most likely French or Spanish. You vaguely remember some of it and you probably even have your old text book around somewhere in the back of the closet or up in the attic. Well, this is a good starting point. Get it out, dust it off, and look it over. Then think about picking up where you left off.

If incentive is what you need, how about planning a trip to a country where that language is spoken? No better place to try out those new phrases than the actual country of origin.

If your budget is tight, there's another interesting alternative: foreign magazines and books. No, not the dreary literature they made you study in college. No wonder you ran screaming out of the classroom. I mean junk, gossip, murder mysteries, fun stuff. Nothing will motivate you quite as much as desperately needing to figure out who really done it.

I brushed up my French by plowing through a couple of George Simenon's detective novels. They are short, easy to understand, and he wrote several hundred of them. They are the French answer to Agatha Christie and lots of fun to read.

Admittedly, I struggled through the first one. But it got easier and after a dozen of these fun little novels, my brain is now a virtual storehouse of French police and forensic terminology!

And if novels, albeit popular ones, still seem too heavy, go for the magazines. Read the ads or read the gossip!

Foreign countries have movie stars, too, and, of course, they love to rattle on about our movie stars as well. You can find foreign publications these days at some of the large bookstores, the so-called superstores.

You can even read the foreign magazines over coffee without paying for them and then slip them back on the rack when you're done. (Assuming you are that kind of person, and I am.)

Finally my personal take on difficulty levels. If you want an easy-to-learn language, go for Spanish or Italian. Both are very logically laid out and the words sound like they are written. In my opinion, German is more difficult and French is every bit as bad as English in terms of irregularity, weird spellings, and idiomatic phrases. Having said that, I can tell you that French is my personal love.

You see, sometimes you find that a language just calls you. Maybe because your ancestors came from a place where that language was spoken. Or maybe you just have an affinity for a particular culture and a yearning to understand their language.

Whatever the reason, curiosity and interest will certainly help stretch your brain enough to embrace a second set of words and sounds.

You've nothing to lose and everything to gain from the experience. Persevere, stretch your brain. It's wonderful exercise.

EXERCISE

4

Stretch and Open Your Mind

Probably the very worst consequence of letting your brain go largely unexercised is its tendency to become narrowed.

And if you stay in a rut long enough, it starts to feel like the express track. Since you're moving forward and at a nice high rate of speed, you stop noticing that you have lost control of the direction in which you are going.

While it may feel comfortable to let your brain view all problems in the same old way, it is nonetheless inefficient and limiting.

The world changes and problems that we thought we had already solved have a nasty habit of reappearing in new forms. It's rather like those pesky viruses. Problems mutate, too. Fortunately, our minds have the ability to keep up with this annoying tendency.

You may not be able to teach an old dog new tricks, but you can most certainly teach an old brain just about anything. That is, as long as the brain remains open and receptive to new thoughts and new ideas.

Brain Stretches • **147**

The main difficulty is our tendency to unilaterally "decide" at some point that a problem is solved. It may not be, but we don't care anymore. We are tired of hearing about it and do not want to have to look at it again. So it is over, done, leave me alone.

This no doubt accounts for the declining voter turnouts in our political elections. Our poor tired brain is thinking something like this, "Hey, didn't we already elect somebody and didn't they say they were going to fix that problem? What? It's still not done and now I have to listen to someone else tell me what they are going to do about it? Oh, let's just forget it, can we?"

At least that's how my brain reacts. It takes a tremendous effort for me to talk it into listening one more time. Why do I do it? Because deep down I know that the dimensions of the problem have undoubtedly changed. It's not really the same problem that it was and the solution I worked out before is no longer valid. I know that because that's the way life works. It changes and, much as I hate it, I know that my brain is better off changing with it.

Now the good news. We are not alone. Everyday, young fresh minds come along and get right to work trying to solve the problems of the world. They have boundless energy and some new approaches, which means they could actually come up with an answer that our brains haven't yet thought of.

"To change your mind and follow him who sets you right is to be nonetheless the free agent that you were before."—*Marcus Aurelius*

The problem is, we have to listen and pay attention in order to determine if these new brains actually do have something worthwhile to add. And then there's always the very real danger that our brains might be asked to let go of some cherished if outdated notions. Brains don't do that easily, even if it is good for them.

Okay, so if flexibility really is a necessary element in a healthy happy brain, how do we get our brains to maintain this flexibility?

Very simple. We keep our minds as open as possible. We practice listening to new ideas, to contrary ideas, even to ideas we've heard before and strongly disagree with.

We listen and attempt to temporarily suspend judgment.

In fact, we even attempt to get inside that other point of view and see what it feels like. We try this different thinking on just like we might try on a pair of shoes at a store.

And remember, just as when we're shopping, we are under no obligation to buy.

The goal here is not to change our minds, or even necessarily to modify our positions. All we really want to do is to stretch our minds. Allow our brain to consider a totally different point of view.

And this process can often pay strange dividends. Considering the opposite point of view from the one we hold often sparks a third, entirely new thought in our brain; a thought that has nothing to do with either our old way of thinking or with the idea that we were considering.

Ah, now you're catching on! This is one of the ways original thinking comes about, through consideration of possibilities that our brains at first find strange, wrong, and even silly. In the process of trying to make sense, sometimes our brains actually reach a deeper and more profound understanding of the problem. (This process is the very basis of scientific inquiry. Check out the chapter on professional exercises to see how a scientist goes about warming up the old noodle.)

So, how do we package this into a regular and doable exercise?

Easy. We start by paying open-minded attention anytime a debate erupts around us.

Next time you're part of a discussion or argument, try to step back and listen before you dive in with your own two cents. Ask questions, draw out the position, and do it honestly and in a friendly and courteous manner.

People can best express their ideas and positions if they feel they are getting a fair hearing. This means that even if you totally disagree with what the other person is saying, let them know you are still willing to hear them out and are willing to mentally "try on" their position.

And when you give your feedback, try to be clear and precise about our own ideas and criticism. And, if at all possible, leave emotion out of the mix.

A first-rate mind uses the power of reason to defend a passion, not the other way around.

If you live in a community of absolute harmony and never experience conflict, then go seek it out. Try going to a local community meeting. No shortage of arguments there. Or try attending a political meeting, particularly one from a party you disagree with.

Another good one is to attend a religious service of a different faith, try to understand what it is they believe and hold to be important.

You can also practice your open mind just listening to speakers on television programs. Assuming, that is, that you listen to people you disagree with. That's really the key. You must listen to all sorts of different, even bizarre ideas if you are to stimulate your brain and stretch it out.

Remember, the brain needs a constant flow of fresh information in order to prosper.

So filter out whatever you don't want to retain after it goes in, not before. Trust your judgment process to weed out bad and flabby ideas.

After all, your brain is one of the best, isn't it?

CHAPTER 11

A Brain Exercise
for the Couch Potato

How To Channel Surf Your Neurons into Fabulous Shape!

Find yourself spending way to much time basking in the phosphorus glow of that old seductive boob tube?

A critic once described television as "bubble gum for the eyes." It would have been more accurate to have said "bubble gum for the brain."

Still, ordinary network television can provide the motivation for a very useful exercise. Don't believe it?

Well, here's an interesting brain exercise that actually requires that you turn on the television and tune in to your favorite program. (And, yes, you can even snack while doing it.)

EXERCISE

The Exercise

1

Beginner

Ready? Got your remote in hand? Okay, here's what you do.

Turn on your favorite sitcom, drama, or soap opera. A half-hour is easiest, but if you really want to fire up those neural circuits, go for a full one-hour show.

Now, pay close attention (except to the commercials) because, yes, there will be a quiz.

As soon as the program is over, turn off the set (I know that's the hard part) and focus your mind on what you just saw.

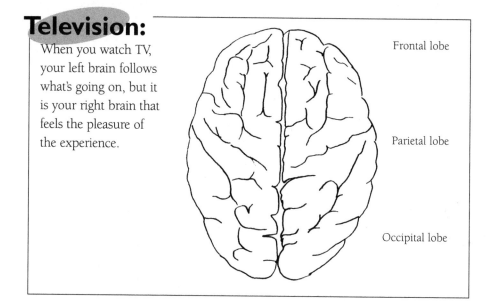

Television:

When you watch TV, your left brain follows what's going on, but it is your right brain that feels the pleasure of the experience.

Frontal lobe

Parietal lobe

Occipital lobe

Start with the opening scene and run through, in your mind, exactly what happened. Try to recall who spoke the first line and what they said. Try to recall who was in the first scene, where it was it taking place, the time of day—everything you can. Just start a running description of the show in the order in which it occurred.

If at all possible, do the exercise out loud. Pretend you are explaining what happened to someone who has not seen the program. Put in as much detail as you can remember, including actual dialogue. If you're up to it, you can even try to duplicate the delivery of the lines and the accents.

Choose your descriptive words carefully. Attempt to describe everything that you remember as lucidly, as concisely, and as completely as you can.

Take small breaks whenever you come to a commercial if you like, but try to go all the way through the show.

Now, most likely, you will leave some parts out and then suddenly remember them after you have moved on. You may also suddenly realize that you reversed a scene or a couple of lines. Don't worry and don't go back. Just file the information in your mind or, if you like, make written notes as you go.

Okay, when you are finished with the last scene, the last line, take a break. Have a soda or a snack and wait fifteen minutes.

You may look over any notes you made during this break.

Now, tell the story again, and this time try to be even more accurate. Go through the whole show, tell your invisible listener everything you can. Try to capture the humor, the drama. Try to be a first class storyteller.

Okay, that's the complete exercise. Second time through, you are done.

Do this exercise at least once a week for six weeks.

This exercise will benefit your brain in several ways. First of all, it will (dare I say it?) dramatically improve your event memory. But it will also greatly improve your powers of observation and explanation.

"I don't think necessity is the mother of invention— invention, in my opinion, arises directly from idleness, possibly also from laziness."—Agatha Christie

And, as an added bonus, you will become indispensable to those friends of yours who were sweating themselves silly at the gym and sadly forgot to set their VCRs for the new episode of "Frasier."

Speaking of which, you may of course tape the episode you watched and then check yourself for accuracy when you're done with your exercise.

For an advanced version of this exercise, actually write the story down on paper. Try to duplicate the original script if you can.

Not only will you benefit in the ways mentioned above, but you will also be learning how television scripts are put together.

I know several successful script writers, particularly comedy writers, who began studying their craft by doing a version of this exercise.

You may find it rather interesting to see what a joke or a gag line looks like written down. And once you have a line on paper, you can play with it. Try changing a word, maybe improve on the phrasing. You might even come up with a better line. Who knows; you may have a hidden talent. This is a great way to find out.

CHAPTER 12

HOW THE PROS EXERCISE THEIR BRAINS

Ways You Can Use Their Techniques to Sharpen up Your Own Synapses.

Human beings seem to have come up with more ways to earn their living than just about all the other animals combined.

And unlike most of the other animals, who sometimes seem to be in an awful rut, we humans just love to keep thinking up new and different things we can do using our brains. Half the time we don't seem to care if what we are doing results in earning a living, just as long as it is interesting and fun.

But, clever folks that we are, we have also taken just about everything we know how to do including playing perfectly useless games like baseball and turned them into bona fide, wage-earning professions. (Just try to imagine a bunch of giraffes organizing a sports franchise and getting other giraffes to kick in their hard-earned twigs and leaves to watch!)

Okay, so we humans like to specialize in what we do. And we like to use our brains in all sorts of unusual ways. We like to call ourselves things like artists, engineers, doctors, salespeople, and, yes, baseball players. All of these things are, of course, professions. But some of these professions require special kinds of brain activity that we call talent.

It would appear that talent is something inborn, given to the fortunate few, leaving the rest of us sadly lacking. And, not being born with a natural talent or "gift," we ordinary folk just assume that we are incapable of similar mental performance.

But do people with talent really have some brain circuits that the rest of us are missing? Do you need special kinds of synapse configurations to think up musical tunes or write novels or understand physics?

And how about throwing a fast ball at a target sixty feet away with uncanny accuracy? Is that simply an inborn talent, something the rest of us can never do no matter how hard we try?

Well, I would certainly say that you need to be born with a talented arm in order to throw a baseball ninety plus miles an hour. However, throwing a baseball with accuracy is something that a great number of us can learn to do. It's a basic coordination skill that can be developed, particularly in the young.

Okay, but how about the other things like writing music, being a painter, or thinking like a scientist? These are also mental abilities that all of us possess to some degree. These skills, talents, gifts, or whatever you want to call them, collectively belong to the human race. All of us have them. Some of us are indeed more "naturally" adept than others, but the latent ability is there in all of us. How these mental skills manifest themselves is often just a question of how we develop and use them and more importantly how *much* we use them.

While we may not all be untapped geniuses, we all possess much more skill and talent than we realize. I promise you we can all do things mentally that we don't know we can do.

And often, people don't realize the stuff they have tucked away inside their skulls, all those secret and hidden abilities, simply because they don't know how to tap into them. They don't have access because they don't know how to reach out and wiggle those circuits, get them activated. They never learned how to turn them on, get them up and running.

Often a person's "discovery" of a special skill or talent happens accidentally. They simply stumble over it one day while playing with their brain. They didn't know they could do it until they actually did it.

Sadly, the reverse is more common. People live their entire life not knowing about a latent talent. Now that is a tragedy.

Okay, so what good does this knowledge do you now, all you undiscovered composers, architects, novelists, and major league hurlers? To be honest, if you're an athlete and your time has passed, I'm afraid you're probably out of luck.

But, if you have some other untapped mental ability, the news may be good. Your talent may still be bankable even if you've already reached your golden years. (But don't wait too much longer.)

Of course, I can't promise that the world at large will appreciate your newly discovered mental prowess and deem you worthy of prizes and accolades. Still, you may find it satisfaction enough to finally just scratch that itch that has been bothering you for all these years and say to yourself, "You know, I always had a feeling I could do something like that. And now I know I can!"

For those of you who probably need a little mental shaping up before embarking on your new career, I list below a series of brain exercises that professionals in various fields use to light up those circuits that they hold most dear.

I also try to show those of you who aren't going to turn into a Stravinsky or Stephen King, how doing some of the exercises the pros use can be beneficial in your everyday, unprofessional life.

So, if you want to be a writer, singer, actor, filmmaker, here's the stuff that helps to make it happen, brain-wise. And if you are more logically inclined, the key to scientific thinking is also hereby revealed.

Writers, Creative and Otherwise

The word writer is really a bit of a misnomer. Writers are really just storytellers who, for convenience, use a written language to put their stories down on paper. (It also makes distribution and royalty collection much, much easier.)

So if you want to be a creative writer or even a nonfiction writer, you will benefit by doing some brain exercise that enhances and improves your storytelling circuits.

And even if you don't fantasize about winning the Pulitzer prize, think about this. Nearly all human communication, oral and written, is packaged in the form of a story.

Stories get told every time two or more human beings meet. We all love to hear a good story and we all have an inherent ability for this most basic human skill.

So we can all benefit from doing some exercise to improve on this wonderful gift we all share.

And remember, creative endeavors like writing are not just about talent or gifts. It may surprise you to learn that many professional writers took up the craft because they thought they weren't very good at telling stories and wanted to get better at it. Exercise can and will improve your native ability whatever it is.

I'm going to tell you about two basic storytelling exercises that I personally have done since I was a child.

Interestingly, for years I didn't recognize them as brain exercises, exercises pretty much essential to the craft of creative writing.

I used to think they were just some quirky things I did. But as I came to know more and more writers, I discovered that all of them did pretty much the same exercises. The form varied, but the content and the purpose were always the same.

Oddly enough, like me, many of them didn't even realize they were doing exercises. They thought they were just "goofing around."

I've come to believe these exercises are probably as old as the profession itself.

There are two basic exercises involved in storytelling or writing because there are two basic brain systems involved.

The first has to do with event memory and the second with imagination.

EXERCISE
1

Exercising a Writer's Memory

A writer needs a good memory. You can't very well tell a story if you can't remember it.

And it's true even if you plan to write the story down as you make it up. After all, you need to be able to hold on to the details at least long enough to get them on paper, and, in truth, most writer's have to "mull over" the story in their mind for some time before beginning the actual writing process.

Besides that, if you're a fiction writer or a journalist, describing what people say and do is your bread and butter. Which brings me to the all-important subject of eavesdropping, a favorite pastime of writers and one of the most valuable ways to collect ideas and material.

Here again, memory is paramount.

You see, most people don't like the idea of some stranger—or worse—friend taperecording or writing down what they are saying. The solution is, of course, to have a crackerjack memory so that you can later recall anything overheard that interests you. How do you do this? You exercise, of course.

And how do writers specifically exercise their memory? Much the same as we did in one of the short-term memory exercises. Writers practice recalling recent events, conversations they have overheard, scenes they have witnessed, sometimes even a movie or a television show they have recently seen. (After all, it's good to know what the competition is doing and you never know when you might find something you can steal.)

This exercise comes very naturally to writers. They usually do the work daily, often when they have a free moment and there is nothing interesting going on to observe. They tune out the world and switch on their event-memory circuits. Then, in their mind, they begin to rerun some recent conversation or event that has interested them.

And if nothing terribly interesting has happened recently, they will just rerun some trivial or mundane event, like a conversation with a checkout clerk at the supermarket.

The exercise matters more than the event. So, in a pinch, just about anything that happened will do.

In this exercise, the writer strives to recall not only the words, but also the visuals of the event, how the individuals looked, what they were wearing, their mannerisms, their accents—anything and everything about what took place. They might try to recall the background, what the room looked like, the sounds, the smells.

Some days they attempt to recall a scene in great detail. Other days, they will simply try to recall and freeze out an overall image or mood that the event evoked for them.

It's all about sharpening up the memory circuit and this exercise definitely does the trick. It's a good workout and it can be done anytime, anywhere.

(In a variation of this exercise, some writers like to practice describing the scene with full sentences and prose. They actually test out different possibilities for the retelling. This cleverly combines memory exercise with a direct craft exercise and is something I find most writers eventually discover and do as well.)

After the workout, the vividly recalled scene is often thrown away, the words and images discarded. Still, every once in awhile, in the midst of a creative project, some long-ago memory exercise might just flash into the writer's mind and become the basis for a wonderful scene or an interesting character.

Clearly this kind of exercise can pay off in more ways than one.

Okay, so the value of this kind of an exercise for a professional writer is obvious, but what about us ordinary folks?

Well, if you will take the trouble to sit yourself down a couple of times a week and try to recall the dialogue and events you overhear in your everyday life, it can benefit you in several different ways.

First and foremost, it's a really fun way to improve your overall event memory. Second, you'll find, perhaps surprisingly, that your descriptive powers will be greatly enhanced by this recall exercise. You see your "mind's eye" will become more adept at holding onto and "freezing" mental pictures so that you can more easily pick out the details that you wish to recall and convey.

Next, you will find the exercise improves your ability to recall spoken dialogue with great precision. And that means you can safely trust important information or instructions to your memory alone. (Look maw, no paper!) What a great confidence booster that is!

Lastly, should you harbor a secret desire to someday finally write that novel, you know that your "writer's memory" will be all fired up and ready to go!

EXERCISE

2

Exercising a Writer's Imagination

Even if you are trying to write a factual story, you will need to use your imagination to frame the story and give it a point of view. In fact, I sometimes think so-called nonfiction requires much more imagination than fiction.

The imagination exercise that a writer does bears striking similarities to the kinds of exercises creative scientists use as well. That's because all human imagination begins with same thing, curiosity.

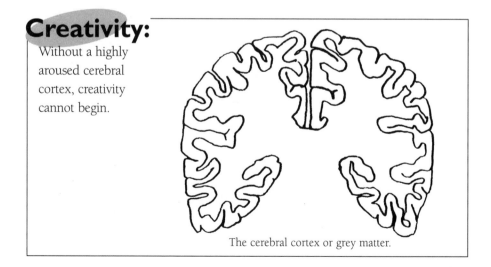

Creativity:
Without a highly aroused cerebral cortex, creativity cannot begin.

The cerebral cortex or grey matter.

Now, you've been told that curiosity killed the cat, but don't forget it has also made quite a few of our species extremely rich. Curiosity drives invention—whether it be a better mousetrap (sorry, pussy cat) or the next best-selling thriller. The way we use our curiosity shapes our creative endeavors.

The creative writer's curiosity almost always centers around some form of human behavior. (Even science fiction and fantasy stories have human-like behavior in them, otherwise we wouldn't be able to relate to them.)

So the writer's exercise period generally involves human questions and problems. Basically things humans do. Where do they come from? From observation and personal experience.

Much like the memory exercise, this exercise starts with an event. The event can be one that was witnessed or read about or even just freely imagined. It doesn't matter, just as long as it evokes the writer's curiosity. But unlike the memory exercise, here the goal is not just to recall the event but to embellish it.

Again, during periods of quiet, a writer will find a warm comfy spot and begin thinking about the event he or she has chosen for the exercise period.

"It is better to know some of the questions than all of the answers."—James Thurber

The writer will generally start thinking with phrases like "What if…" or "Just suppose for a minute…," then let his or her imagination roam, very much like a freeform daydream. At first, the writer will avidly follow whatever possibilities spring to mind. The scene may move or be transformed to a new location. New people may enter, hidden motives may surface, heck, spaceships might even land! Whatever the imagination wants, the imagination gets, at least for a while.

But unlike a pure daydream, the writer will be subtly directing this guided daydream by occasionally reinterjecting variations of those starting questions, "Now what if...?" or "Okay, suppose after that, this were to happen...." The imagination is allowed a wide latitude only until something interesting is spotted.

Then the writer begins to direct the imagination more narrowly, like a bloodhound on a scent. If he or she feels game's afoot, a possible story, then the writer's mind undergoes a subtle change. He or she begins to treat the imagined scene just like a remembered scene and tries to milk out every possible detail. (Now you see why the memory exercise is so important.)

The session might go on for hours. If the writer has the freedom, maybe even all day or over several days. It's a transfixing experience and a wonderful high. And, yes, I believe it is probably addicting, at least if you truly are a writer.

What results from this exercise is a story. Many times, perhaps most of the time, one of no great consequence.

The excitement often fades when the details of the imagined story are examined in the cold light of day. Alas, it wasn't great art after all. But it sure was fun, and the writer knows that if this exercise is done regularly, sooner or later, there will be a payoff.

An Exercise for an Actor

If you've ever known a professional actor then you know that the jokes about them are true. Most of them are always, as they say in the trade, "on." What that means is that they never seem to stop playing a role. It's just in their nature, or is it?

Actually it's a way of sharpening their craft, keeping their neural circuits tuned up.

The annoying part is when they keep jumping around, playing different parts or doing different accents according to random cues at the dinner table. But other times they do it in a more focused and serious way. And you know what? We all do it, just not as much.

Haven't you ever tried a different accent, or tried to mimic someone's way of speaking? Ah, you see, Shakespeare was right! All the world is a stage. Unfortunately, it's populated with too many lousy actors. So if you want to improve your standing, here are some tips.

EXERCISE

3

Improvisation

We all know what improvisation is and we all appreciate people who are practiced and skilled at it.

Professional actors improvise all the time. They sometimes take on an improvised role for an entire day or even several days. They usually do it to practice for an upcoming role, or at least that's what they say if you catch them at it. You see, the safest way to improvise is in front of strangers who presumably don't realize you are just pretending. Here's an example.

An actor might take on say, a deep Southern accent. Everywhere he or she goes, stores, restaurants, bus stops, wherever, they put on a Southern accent and demeanor. They might even pretend to be a visitor from the South. They would then make every attempt to engage in small conversations with people they meet during the course of the day. They get to practice the accent and it also gives them a chance to see how they are doing. If they notice a puzzled look on the person they are talking to, then they realize they have sounded a false note. They will try to correct it with the next victim.

Sometimes actors do these routines in twos or threes, each one of them trying something different. Other times it's an ensemble. It lets them practice their craft and it's also fun. Actors love to have fun. That's one of their good points.

Now variations on this include simply pretending to be in a mood that is not real. For example, looking sad at a bar to see if it evokes sympathy. Or maybe they'll try being ridiculously happy and full of cheer just to see if they can get people to react to them. It's called engaging the audience.

I even knew of one actor who, while playing the part of a death-row inmate, got dressed up in his costume, went out to a biker's bar and convinced a group of tough-looking thugs that he had just gotten out of jail that day and was hellbent to settle a score with the cop who had put him in. Believe it or not, these tough guys did their best to calm him down and talk him out of the idea. Apparently he evoked enough empathy, they genuinely didn't want to see him go back to the slammer.

Okay, what I have described so far is fairly blunt. The truth is that good actors more often than not try on very subtle characters and accents. They are looking to hone, not chop.

So, what good does this do us? After all, we're not professional or even amateur actors.

As stated above, according to the Bard, you are indeed an actor. We all have to act in our daily lives, most often at our place of work. The difference is that we usually act defensively, that is, we try to screen off what we are really thinking for protection. After all, if the boss really knew what you thought of him, you'd be out of a job faster than a bad actor.

But you can use this same natural talent in a positive way. You can pretend to be more assertive or more positive or just more cheerful for the purpose of furthering your position.

And you can "try on" your stronger or more positive behavior around town before letting it loose in the office.

If you feel you are not forceful enough or don't speak up for yourself as much as you should, try practicing on a sales clerk. (No rudeness or browbeating now, I mean positive, strong behavior.)

The same could be true if people tell you that you are too abrasive or abrupt. Want to try to be more sensitive? Try it with strangers first. Strike up a sensitive conversation with someone in a chance encounter or back to that famous sales clerk.

See how people respond to your new act. Sharpen it, tune it, and when you are ready, take it on the road!

Brain waves:

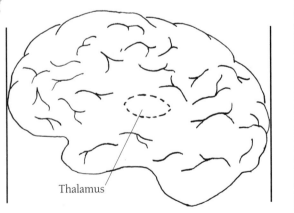

An electromagnetic wave pulses back and forth across the brain every 12.5 thousands of a second. This may be how sensory and other information is synchronized. The thalamus is believed to initiate the wave.

Thalamus

A 40 hertz wave is constantly sweeping the brain

Musicians and a Sound Exercise

Most musicians get plenty of exercise just doing what they do. In fact, reading and playing music and especially sight-reading is some of the best overall brain exercise you can get.

But those darn musicians are never satisfied. They're always coming up with more stuff to challenge their already well-oiled neurons (at least as compared to mine).

Here's one exercise some musical friends of mine do effortlessly. I, of course, have yet to get past the first line, but I stubbornly keep trying. See if you can do better.

EXERCISE

4

The exercise is deceptively simple. Take a well-known song, such as "The Star Spangled Banner." You are going to sing the song, but there is, of course, a catch. You begin singing the song on first note but the second, not the first word.

So instead of starting out with the phrase, "Oh, say, can you see..." you start out, "Say, can you see by the...." Every word is exactly one off from where it normally falls in the music.

Sounds easy until you try it. You can also do it the other way and start with the last word, "brave? Oh, say, can you...."

The odd thing is, it's very easy to do if you don't know the song. It's the fact that our brain is expecting a correlation that makes it so hard. The more familiar the song, the more difficult the exercise is.

Musicians love this one because it shakes things up in their musical circuits, gets them out of a neural rut. They toss it right off. Unfortunately, it just makes me aware of how locked in my poor music nets really are.

Try the exercise if you can. I'll give you a small hint. It is somewhat easier if you write the words down on paper and read them as you try to sing what can only be described as lopsided. Good luck.

Artists, How They Draw as Opposed to How We Draw

Artists most often exercise by sketching or drawing. They draw objects or groups of objects that catch their eye and interest them. They also draw things they see in their imagination. It's a useful and enviable skill. One that comes in handy when you're trying to explain how something looks.

Now, we can all draw to some degree. If I asked you to draw a square, you'd say no problem. You could easily do that. In fact, if I asked you to draw a cube, you could probably add the five extra lines to your square and make a pretty good approximation. Still no problem.

But what if I asked you to draw something real, some object sitting in the room? You might not feel quite so confident. Drawing an imaginary object is a whole lot easier than trying to copy something we can actually see.

Why? Because we don't use our eyes and memory the way an artist does. To draw something, an artist examines an object long enough to actually create a mental image in their mind of how the object looks. He or she then simply visualizes that mental image on a piece of paper. Making the drawing is just a matter of tracing the image. Sound simple? For a simple outline drawing, it actually is.

EXERCISE 5

Try this little exercise. Look at a small object nearby, something with a simple shape. Mentally draw a line around the perimeter. Now squint your eyes and just see the outline you have drawn.

Close your eyes and hold onto the image. Now, look at a blank white piece of paper and superimpose the outline image that's there in your mind. Now trace it with a pencil. If you lose the mental image, look at the object again and then come back to the paper. That's how artists do it. We amateurs try to look at both at once. That's much harder because your brain is then called upon to do a scale conversion between the two images. Not easy.

If you have a more complex object, you break it down into easily studied parts. You might do a rough overall outline and then focus on the details one at time. You would transfer each piece to your paper individually with the outline providing you with a location just like a map. To become skilled, it's just a matter of practice. The more you do it, the better you get. And anybody can learn.

Besides possibly turning you into a fanatical sketch artist, this exercise can also greatly improve your ability to remember what objects look like. The next time you see a household object in a store that you like and may want to buy, try mentally sketching it. Then go home and mentally place it where you want to use it. As you can see, this can be a very useful skill.

By the way, the more your brain likes something, the easier it is to remember and the easier it is to draw. That's why artists always prefer to draw what they like, not what their patrons necessarily want.

Pictures That Move

If you wonder what sort of exercise a filmmaker does to keep his or her brain going strong, the answer is they do exercises very similar to writers, only different.

Part of that difference lies in the fact that motion pictures are often a secondary art. The source material is mostly likely to be a short story, a novel, or a true story.

So the filmmaker's mental exercise consists of taking the primary story and converting it into a series of (hopefully) connected images, a film.

The outward exercise is not unlike a writer's memory exercise except that a translation is taking place from a written script. Each remembered scene (remembered from reading the story) has to be both visualized and dramatized. The filmmaker must get his or her mind to step sequentially through a series of mental images that will comprise the scene.

Now sometimes the dramatization is done by a scriptwriter, but the visualization is entirely up to the filmmaker.

And if that isn't enough, the filmmaker has to cope with dialogue, camera movement, sound effects, and even special effects. Why do all this astounding mental work? Because the filmmaker needs to hold in his or her mind the total image of the film before it is ever made.

The script contains only thumbnail descriptions, ultimately you can't write down pictures.

Often the filmmaker is the only person who actually has any idea what the film is going to look like. That's why studio heads pull their hair out and that's why the exercises take on great importance. They are not just mental preparation, they are the actual work.

Now to be fair, the exercises are usually done in layers. A filmmaker is unlikely to be able to immediately visualize the final product.

The exercise is done repeatedly. The film is seen again and again, each time adding detail until finally a storyboard can be worked out and the elaborate and expensive process of actually shooting can begin.

We all do a mini-version of this process when we plan out our day in the morning. We "see" ourselves going though a series of motions, and appearing at various locations for various reasons.

But we are usually not very detailed in our minds and our images are somewhat foggy and incomplete. If we learn to imagine more precisely and more accurately, our film-making can pay off in the ability to foresee problems and anticipate needs.

If we visualize our actions carefully, we often suddenly remember something we were about to overlook. We must not forget to take the camera or the umbrella or the all-important report. Or we anticipate that we are going to need more cash and then visualize in our mind where we remember seeing a convenient ATM. A very handy skill and all it takes is focus and practice.

So while you may not want to try your hand at Hollywood, keep your own film factory working well, even if you are only making documentaries.

Scientific Thinking

People think of a scientific brain as a brain that loves highly complex thoughts and ideas. Actually, the opposite is true. Scientists love simplicity. They spend their time not just trying to discover the laws of nature, but lobbying to get those laws simplified as much as possible. Just like a certain political party, they hate the idea of excessive government.

When scientists speak of a theory as being "elegant" (which is one of their favorite words), they mean that the theory breaks down into simple rules that any ordinary brain like mine can understand. That's when they know they've got something hot, something they can actually sell.

So scientists, just like the rest of us, really do like it simple. If they could, they would gladly leave complexity to the artists and the Democrats.

The other interesting thing about scientific brains is the way they start the thinking process.

Scientists just ask questions, usually very simple, seemingly obvious questions, like "Why is the sky blue?" or "Why is the sun hot?"

"To be conscious that you are ignorant is a great step to knowledge."—Benjamin Disraeli

Sometimes those simple questions take hundreds of years and a lot of complicated research to figure out. Other times, with a really clever scientific brain, a seemingly impossible question turns out to have a simple (or as a scientist would say "elegant") solution, one any ordinary person could verify.

My favorite example is the problem posed by the cosmologically huge question, "Is the universe infinite in time and space?" which can be answered, surprisingly, by simply walking out into your backyard, looking up at the stars, and asking yourself another question, "Why is the night sky dark?"

You see, if the universe really were infinite, meaning it went on forever, then all the light from that infinity of stars would have been shining through space forever as well. And all that light from all those stars would fill up all the space in the universe and the night sky would be as bright as day. Since the night sky is dark, the universe can't possibly be infinite. Case closed.

So, you see, scientists don't just think in powers of ten and strange-looking calculus formulas. They actually try, whenever possible, to keep things simple. They just can't always pull it off. But for that matter, neither can the rest of us.

So what does a scientific brain do for exercise? It just asks a simple question and then tries to answer it. That usually leads to enough exercise for a good ten ordinary lifetimes.

So what can we take from scientific thinking?

We can benefit by understanding that the solution to a problem often comes through a process of asking ourselves a series of questions. Scientists understand that questions are really just a simplified way of stating the problem, a way of reducing it to a manageable thought with which the brain can cope.

"He who would be cured of ignorance must confess it."—Michel Eyquem de Montaigne

You actually take a problem apart, dissect it with questions, and arrive at the solution by finding the correct questions to ask. Einstein once said that if he had a talent, a skill, a genius that set him a part from other scientists and other men, it was the ability to know exactly what question to ask. Because once you've got the right set of questions, the answer becomes obvious.

The Well-Exercised Brain of an Athlete

Top athlete's like to talk about getting their brain into the "flow." What they mean by that is getting the brain into a state of high concentration where it is completely focused on just one task. Everything else in the world is shut out and ignored.

The reason they do this is because success in big time sports has become a question not so much of who has the bigger physical talent, but who has the best concentration.

To hone the body's reflexes to respond in hundredths of a second (near the limit of potential) requires that the brain not fire one unnecessary neuron. A single stray or wayward signal could make the difference between returning a one-hundred-and-twenty-mile-an-hour serve and being aced. In the case of a major league hitter facing a hard-throwing reliever, it could literally mean serious injury, even death.

So how do athletes get into the "flow" and what is the "flow" anyway? The flow is type of trance state, not unlike being hypnotized. In fact, it probably is a form of self-hypnotism. The brain zones in on a task and everything else fades into the background.

André Agassi, the tennis player, once stated in an interview that when he was in the "flow" all he was aware of was a moving yellow-green ball. He didn't hear or see the crowd. He didn't hear or see his opponent. All he saw was that ball coming toward him and all his mind was thinking about was the action of meeting it with the racket. Other athletes speak in much the same terms.

In the case of runners, the "flow" is sometimes described more as a kind of "high," which some researchers believe is the result of the body releasing endorphins into bloodstream.

Cerebellum:

The cerebellum controls delicate and skilled motion. The split second timing of a hockey goalie, the balance of a dancer, and the trained hand of a sugeon all originate here.

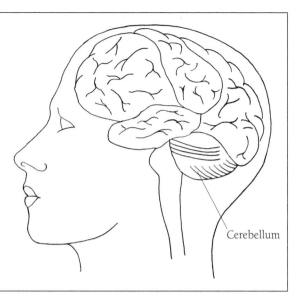

Cerebellum

But the feeling of being of one purpose, of being single-minded is also present.

It's this highly focused state that allows peak performance, whether you are running a marathon or hitting a tennis ball or collapsing down in front of the net trying to stop a slap shot from going through in hockey.

Years ago we used to stereotype athletes as muscle-bound and dull-witted. But we now realize nothing could be further from the truth. A successful athlete must also have a superb brain. In fact, the brain of the athlete is as important as his or her physical ability, if not more so.

So how do they do it, get into the "flow"? Athletes achieve this brain state by focused practice in which they concentrate for hours at a time doing repetitive tasks related to their sport. Their physical and mental exercise periods are superimposed. It's highly economical.

8

How can we benefit?

By using our exercise periods to focus our brains in the same way. Now we can't expect the same physical performance as a professional athlete, but we can certainly match their concentration and get into the "flow" just like the big boys.

All it takes is dedication to purpose and concentrated repetition. If you have trouble achieving this state, try to find a trainer or athlete who can help you learn. You might also want to try the self-hypnosis exercise later in this book to get a sense of what kind of brain state you are trying to achieve.

CHAPTER 13

LEARNING IS EXERCISE

How To Make a Habit of It

The human brain begins the lifelong learning process with birth, if not sooner. (Some people actually believe that the brain may begin collecting information in the womb.)

Throughout our entire lives, our brains continually incorporate new experiences, new information, new skills, new methodology, new ideas. In short, our brains never really stop learning.

However, for all too many of us, the pace of learning slows to a virtual crawl once we have completed our formal schooling and found a comfortable way to earn a living.

"When you're through learning, you're through."
—Vernon Law

Learning is an essential brain function and one that needs to be constantly exercised as much as possible.

The good news is that the brain actually enjoys the stimulation of learning. The bad news is that for too many brains the very word "learning" has taken on an onerous, academic connotation.

Too many brains associate "learning" with the sometimes downright unpleasant "information stuffing" that took place during the long adolescent schooling period.

We were basically required to learn all sorts of factual information that our elders told us was absolutely necessary for our success—if not our very survival.

We found out that while some of the information turned out to be useful, a great deal of it did not, at least not for our particular brain.

Many of us look back on our formal schooling somewhat the way ex-convicts no doubt view their former incarceration, with a mixture of revulsion and perverse pride at having survived the experience. (And, of course, a firm resolution never under any circumstances to return.)

"The only thing more expensive than education is ignorance."—Benjamin Franklin

But learning and formal education are not necessarily synonymous. Formal education is a duty required by society. Learning is a free exploration, a natural process that the brain engages in out of curiosity and a real desire to know.

Learning fuels all the other higher brain functions from problem solving to creativity.

Fortunately, once the formal education cycle is complete, we gain a near absolute freedom to choose what we want our brains to learn or not learn. We can let our brains range free.

The trouble is, too many brains are turned off by the formal experience. They think of learning as something unpleasant, something to be avoided. For those unfortunate brains, learning gets reduced to only what is necessary to earn a living. Basically whatever job training is required of them.

The result is their brains get less and less exercise as their jobs become more and more routine. The learning curve falls off and so does brain activity. Without the constant stimulation of learning, the entire brain grows sluggish. It becomes more and more lethargic and lazy, just like an underused muscle.

To keep those neurons firing, we need to keep learning. But we don't always have to be learning things that we need to know, or are required to know. We can learn things simply because we want to know them, because we are actually interested in the subject matter. After all, we're not in a degree program anymore. No one is trying to force arcane academic subjects down our mental throats.

We can freely choose what we want to learn and that makes all the difference in the world. Learning can finally be just plain fun.

And for those of you who think you are getting all the learning exercise your brain needs because your job requires you to constantly absorb new information (as many jobs do in this brave new world), think about this. Learning required information is not the same thing as the natural process of learning for the sake of curiosity.

A healthy brain also needs learning experiences that fill it with a sense of joy and even, dare I say, wonder. So, unless you absolutely love your job and get all the mental stimulation you can handle, consider doing this exercise.

Okay, so let's lay out a structure for a new kind of learning. Learning that is both good exercise and good fun.

EXERCISE

1

The Exercise

The idea is to turn something that you find interesting into a study course.

We all find something in this world interesting—some subject, some activity.

Perhaps your brain has a yearning to explore some weighty subject like philosophy, art, or science. Or maybe

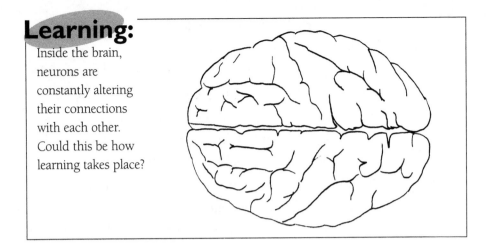

Learning:

Inside the brain, neurons are constantly altering their connections with each other. Could this be how learning takes place?

you follow politics or current affairs, or major issues like the environment and world peace. That's fine for those brains that like large and intense subjects.

But suppose your brain likes equally interesting but less esoteric subjects like sports, movies, or popular music. Or maybe your brain just likes to keep up with the latest information concerning current personalities (I'm trying to find a non-judgmental way to describe gossip).

Whatever it is that truly interests you, the quality of your subject (as judged by others) is of no consequence. It doesn't matter.

I want your brain to get some good learning exercise and the best way to do that is by giving your brain the widest possible latitude. I leave the absolute choice of material entirely up to you and your brain.

The important thing is that you choose a subject that truly interests you, whatever it is. Chose your absolute favorite subject and don't worry how unimportant it may seem to some Mensa club member.

Now instead of getting your daily dose of learning about your passion from the sports or gossip pages of your local newspaper or—okay, let's admit it—from television, you are going to do some genuine research.

Go to the library or bookstore and pick out three books on the subject you love. Three books on sports, three biographies of movie stars, three books on the environment or world peace or even three books on playing computer games. Three books on humor. Three books on great villains. Three books on saints. Three books on the history of food. Whatever your brain finds interesting.

And if your brain is in such bad shape that you don't know what really grabs it, it's time to find out. Browse at the bookstore and if necessary pick three books on three different subjects. Pick whatever seems to catch your interest at the moment. (Yes, you can just pick the three skinniest books if you want.)

Now you may take up to six weeks to do it, but read them all, cover to cover.

"Only one who has learned much can fully appreciate his ignorance."—Louis L'Amour

If you're not an avid reader, you will find reading about something you love an entirely new and interesting experience. Your brain will absorb the information like a sponge seemingly without effort. You may even find yourself rereading some passages of particular interest. You could even find yourself committing facts to memory without anybody asking you to. Gasp!

And, hopefully, you will find that your brain actually wants to go get more books on the subject or on other subjects.

By the way, in case you think you're too old or too set in your ways to expose your brain to some really serious learning, let me tell you the story of my personal physician—

a man with a grandson about to enter college—to give you some idea of his advanced age without betraying the actual number. A few summers ago, he took off from his busy practice and went to England where he enrolled in a summer course in philosophy at Oxford, a subject completely outside his field which was, of course, the whole point. He came back invigorated, his mind sharpened by the challenge, and, as a bonus, his view of the world considerably widened. He plans to go back again someday, maybe this time in Medieval History, who knows?

"In my early days. I was eager to learn and to do things, and therefore I learned quickly."—Sitting Bull

Just remember that you're going to live a long life, so you might as well keep that brain of yours in the best condition you possibly can. Keep exercising it. Keep learning.

CHAPTER 14

THE GAMES WE PLAY—
HOW TO GET MORE OUT OF THEM

There's Much More to Games Than Simple Entertainment.

From childhood through the end of life, our brains like to engage in game playing. There are thousands to choose from. All kinds of games—ranging from the very physical to the purely mental.

And every generation seems to come up with new ones. It sometimes seems as if our brain's appetite for games is insatiable. We all recognize that the games children play are important developmental tools and we actively encourage our children to engage in them. But the benefits of game-playing continue right on through adult life. Game-playing, particularly the more complex and subtle games that adults tend to engage in are not just simple diversions. They are an important mental exercise.

Games engage and stimulate our brains, often more fully than our day-to-day life does. Our brains thrive on challenge and game-playing can offer our brains a relatively safe way to try out different strategies, new ways of thinking, even wild ideas. Games allow us to take mental risks that might prove dangerous in real life.

And the lessons we learn from game-playing spill over into real life, improving everything from our general problem-solving skills to our ability to adapt to new and different situations. Games played with other people are also an important way for us to improve our intuition and emotional reading skills.

Okay, there are thousands of games to chose from. Which ones are the best brain exercise and how do I maximize the benefit?

Depends entirely on what kind of shape your individual brain is in, what it needs, and how you respond to competition. Since I can't answer these questions, instead I am going to give you some general rules for how to get the most out of any game you might choose to play, using a few well-known games as examples.

The Exercises

EXERCISE

1

Solitaire

Games that we play alone, outside of games requiring simple hand-eye coordination skills, are basically mental puzzles.

Solving a puzzle exercises and improves the brain's basic organizational skills. You start with disorder and you finish with order. We solve the puzzle by using our left-brain logic skills in combination with our right-brain pattern-recognizing circuits. At least, that's what we're supposed to be doing.

If you like puzzles, whether they be jigsaw, crossword, or some card game version like solitaire, just remember to make sure that both sides of your brain are actually participating in the process. Look for patterns and then logically sort them into categories and sequentialize them.

It's very good exercise, particularly if your brain is weak on organization. But trying to solve complicated puzzles can also be very frustrating if you aren't used to the process.

My advice in this case is to start with simple puzzles in whatever form and let your brain gain confidence through experience.

Also try different strategies, even if you've already stumbled across methods that seem to get good results. Try something different anyway. Keep trying to see the problem in a new or novel way. Keep it fresh. Don't be afraid to experiment.

Remember the idea is to constantly challenge the brain to do better, to find new and improved solutions. This makes the difference between doing a puzzle as a diversion and doing a puzzle as a brain exercise.

EXERCISE

2

Adversarial

Games in which our brains are challenged by other brains are excellent exercise as long as we do not allow ourselves to be overwhelmed by the experience.

Games involving competition can be counterproductive if we consistently feel overmatched or even undermatched.

"Education is the ability to listen to almost anything without losing your temper or your self-confidence."
—Robert Frost

Winning and losing are really just a kind of snapshot that we take periodically during the exercise in order to gauge our progress. As such, they are meaningful only as very general indicators.

Just remember that the actual goal of competitive game playing is to get good mental exercise, to improve your skill, and to have fun. So seek competition that is matched to your level or slightly above and play friendly games where you can concentrate on your own personal improvement while the other player or players do the same. This is true for physical games of skill as well as purely intellectual games.

EXERCISE

3

One on One

Games that pit one brain directly against another brain are often the most challenging. The best of them are entirely devoid of randomization, except, of course, for those variables that are introduced by the players themselves.

Chief among these types of games is, of course, chess. Chess is a game of strategy. Theoretically, there is always a best strategy in chess, a best possible move if only a player can discover it amidst the trillion or so possibilities. Therefore, the popular image of a great chess player is a person with a

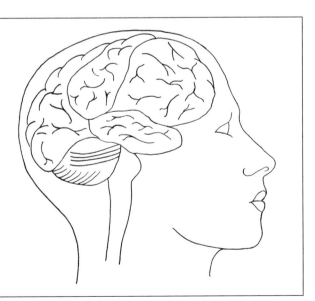

Games:
The frontal lobes mediate our sense of social behavior, our curiosity, and our capacity to realize consequences. Game-playing can exercise all these circuits and more.

highly developed left brain—a cold, calculating genius with incredible powers of logic.

But interestingly enough, the very best chess players are equally adept at pattern recognition, a very right-brained function, which is why, I think, they still maintain a skill advantage over computers programmed to play chess.

Computers, being purely logic machines, merely crunch out several million possible moves, look them all over, and then try to pick the most "logical" one. They can do this at astonishing speeds, far faster than human brains.

But Grand Masters, it seems, don't just rely on logic. They use their whole brains in a still-mysterious process that mixes pattern matching, intuition, and an ability to size up and ultimately predict how an opponent is likely to respond.

That's why they can wax mere beginners like me who tend to think the same way a computer does, logically and sequentially. And since my neural nets can't match the speed of "Big Blue," that's also why it's easy for a computer to beat me, but hard for a computer to beat a Grand Master.

The computer and the Grand Master aren't using the same methodology. So far, the human method has proven superior. Let's hope it stays that way.

So if chess or other less complex games of strategy and logic are your cup of tea, remember that it's not all logic. Patterns, predictions, and intuition about what your opponent might be planning are equally, if not more, important.

So while you are playing, take note of not just your own options and strategies, but try to figure out what your opponent might be planning. Try

Fact: The Grand Master Gary Karpov explained that he was able to ultimately defeat the IBM super-computer "Big Blue" in the Spring of 1996 by studying how the computer "thought" in the first couple of games. Subsequently, he was able to predict what strategy the computer would employ and defeat it rather easily. The computer cannot match this very human ability.

to use your powers of intuition and anticipation so that you exercise your full brain and not just your logic circuits.

Group Games

4

For me, some of the best brain exercise comes from group games, whether they be simple parlor games like charades and dictionary, or very structured games like bridge and Monopoly.

Parlor games not only challenge us to be creative, but we learn from the shared creativity, from watching and learning what others do in similar situations.

"After all, the only proper intoxication is conversation."—Oscar Wilde

In my opinion, one of the best and most fun of these exercises is the game known as "Dictionary."

It's a simple game requiring only a good-sized dictionary and any number of players. Basically a moderator chooses a legitimate word from the dictionary which by consensus is unknown to any of the participating players. (Not as hard as it sounds.) The players then are given pencil and paper and are asked to make up a credible-sounding definition. The moderator writes down the actual definition.

The papers are collected, given numbers for identification and read through twice by the moderator. (Hopefully with a straight face.) The second time through, the players vote for the entry they believe to be the actual definition. Points are awarded to players whose invented definitions draw votes. A point is also given to any player who correctly identifies the true definition. The moderator then rotates so that all may play.

This simple game uses the brain both creatively and deductively. Deception and detection are employed equally along with any intuitive knowledge of how the other players might think. In order to be successful, the brain must be able to match a creative writing sample with the creator. Not easy, but good exercise and a lot of fun.

Tips for this kind of exercise include the advice to concentrate on the task and try not to engage in social defenses.

That is, don't worry yourself about what your opponents might be thinking about the quality of your play. Let your brain plunge in and do it's very best. Remember, some scurrilous players might try to use criticism of your moves as a tactic against you. See it as that and respond accordingly.

This kind of exercise can be very stimulating for the brain and lead you to discover creative thinking you didn't know your brain could do.

EXERCISE

5

Risky Games

Some games involve risk. Physical risk in the case of sports and financial risk when it comes to gambling.

Games involving any kind of risk should be viewed in a similar way. Don't take unprepared risks. Understand the full implications of any risk before you take it. When it comes to risky financial games, remember the first rule of gambling is—be prepared to lose. If you're not prepared to lose, don't play. You won't derive any benefit from the exercise.

That said, the element of possible financial gain or loss seems to have a natural appeal to the brain. The problem involved is one of maintaining a proper perspective. An otherwise rational brain can find itself behaving very irrationally where a large pile of money is concerned. The right brain's desire circuits can flat out overwhelm the Logic circuits resulting in extremely poor decision-making.

Now many of the exercises in this book have been designed to encourage and open up right-brain thinking. Here's one that's just the opposite. It is an exercise in which the left brain must absolutely control, but not still exclude, the right brain. The right brain cannot be totally overridden because it's intuitive input may be critical to success, particularly in the game we are going to discuss, poker.

Poker has many guises and appears outwardly to be a game of chance. But actually poker is a game of money management, of strategy. The correct technical strategy, over time, should succeed. But what makes the game truly interesting is that the apparent correct strategy can be defeated by seemingly irrational play, the famous bluff.

The problem is that the apparent correct strategy is obvious. As such it can be easily recognized and defended against by a skilled player. In order to succeed, a player must disguise his or her strategy by occasionally engaging in an illogical move, a bluff. And since all good players engage in this tactic, a winning player must also be prepared to "call a bluff."

Now before we go sailing off into the depths of poker strategy, let's get back to our main purpose, brain exercise.

To play the game of poker and to derive good exercise from it, you must win more often than you lose. The reason is that unless you are a winning player, you are not properly exercising your brain. In fact you might even be doing a negative exercise, reinforcing weak thinking.

So here's how you become a winning player.

First of all it is crucial that you gain a basic knowledge of the game. You must understand two things about any poker hand you play. What is the average winning hand

and what are the odds of the hand you are holding being a winning hand.

Now you can obtain this knowledge easily from any number of books or, believe it or not, you can just ask during an actual game. Most friendly players will tell you, assuming they know.

In fact, one of the interesting aspects about poker is that many players are actually willing to help educate and train you, even though that training is not in their best financial interest. So if you want to engage in poker as a brain exercise, make sure you know the odds. Next, play with friendly players who are more skilled than you. (But make sure you can afford the stakes.)

Play a strict by-the-odds game and fold often, as this strategy dictates. But after you have folded, pay close attention to how the other players continue to play out the rest of the hand. Use this time to study the art of bluffing and how it is successfully or not successfully employed.

If you pay attention and make sure your right brain behaves and does its job, you can not only get some good exercise, but eventually make a few bucks in the process.

It's your deal.

Physical Games

Physical games can also be very good brain exercise. Many group games emphasize clever strategy and deception just as much as physical prowess.

Softball is a good example. Softball also is a game that provides playing positions for almost every body type. It's even possible for players of mixed skill levels to play together. Each can derive a personal benefit in terms of skill improvement and simple enjoyment, irrespective of the other players.

As with all group or adversarial games, try to keep the brain focused on the object of the game and try not to allow right brain emotions to become overwhelming. Translation, don't get too serious.

Angry or explosive behavior is counterproductive. If you have problems in this area, then here is a good opportunity to work on restraining these right-brain tendencies.

The danger comes when the brain becomes so focused on succeeding that it loses a true sense of perspective. It becomes unable to gracefully accept defeat. Don't let this happen. Remember, it is just exercise, not life and death.

If other players make annoying mental mistakes, remember that it does not reflect on your brain's performance. And if you make mistakes, acknowledge and accept them. Denial robs you of the opportunity to grow. So next time you're out there on the playing field, concentrate hard, play hard, but don't forget to keep control of your feeling circuits.

And don't forget to stretch out both your muscles and mind before you start. Set your goals in your consciousness before you begin actual play. Make sure your brain is as ready as your body.

CHAPTER 15

EXERCISING THE BRAIN'S DREAM AND HYPNOTIC STATES

Do Dream States Have a Practical Use?

We all go to sleep and we all dream. But why do we dream?

Well, if you ask four different dream researchers you will get six different answers.

The truth is that while there is no shortage of theories, no one knows for certain exactly why we dream. It may well turn out that dreaming is not one single brain function but in fact several similar functions, each with a different purpose.

However, we do know that there are several distinct ways in which we can derive benefits from our brain's dreaming process. And best of all we know how to enhance those benefits through simple exercise.

"He hears voices others do not hear, sees visions that confirm his dreams."—Eagle Old Man

What about the so-called trance or hypnotic state?

This is yet another brain function that is recognized, but poorly understood. But entering into a hypnotic or trance state also has very real benefits and like night dreams can be put to good and effective use with a little exercise.

The Exercises

Controlling Unruly Dreams

Before we can effectively use our dreams, we need to gain control over them. This is not as difficult as it may sound.

First of all, you need to realize that dreaming is a semi-conscious, not unconscious, state. You actually have a lot more conscious mind control when you are dreaming than you realize.

The reason you don't necessary feel this control is because the brain, rather wisely I think, shuts down most of the direct motor control circuits. It does this to protect you from taking physical action while in the middle of a dream state, that is in the middle of an imaginary event.

It may well be that our awareness of this physical restraint is what sometimes gives us that terrible feeling of helplessness. And we all know that the panic caused by such a feeling can be great enough to actually awaken us, usually in a cold sweat.

But we can lessen or even avoid this unpleasant experience if we remember that our mind is in fact perfectly free to act and to control the events within our dreams. All we need to do is take over the controls.

Now one unpleasant form of dreaming we are all familiar with is the nightmare. The evidence tends to indicate that bad dreams or nightmares reflect internal conflicts going on inside our brains, usually over some important life events.

Now we don't necessarily want to just stop these from occurring. They clearly have some importance to our psychological health. Rather, the proper way of dealing with them is to resolve the conflict.

Okay, I know you've already spent a fortune on psychotherapy and you are only up to your sixth grade gym teacher, so I'm not going to suggest that you spend more money. It's actually much simpler than that.

"Have a vision not clouded by fear."—The Cherokee

The key to banishing a nightmare (and very likely to resolving the internal conflict) is to take action.

What do I mean by that? I mean, you must gain control over this unpleasant dream. You do this by first of all telling yourself that it is only a dream and a necessary one at that. If it is a recurring dream then tell yourself several times a day and most importantly just before you go to sleep that it is only a dream. It is a natural and harmless event. Tell yourself that you will no longer stand by and be a passive participant. Banish your fear. You can not be harmed in a dream except by letting yourself be frightened. The events, the monsters, the gym teacher, they are all phantoms and more importantly phantoms under your control. That's the good news. You can actually change the course of what is going to happen. You can rewrite the dream.

Think carefully before you go to sleep how you want the situation to come out. Perhaps you pull out your sword and cut the monster's head off or perhaps you just give it a good sound thrashing with your fists. Or let's say you are a pacifist at heart. Then give the monster a verbal thrashing. Tell it to leave you alone. Insist it leave you alone. Send it packing. Do this consciously before you go to sleep.

Now when and if the dream comes, work hard to bring these thoughts, this plan, back into consciousness and take action. If you fail and the dream frightens you and wakes you up, take heart, all is not lost. Gather your strength, maybe

Dreams:

When we dream, brain scans show that the thalamus becomes very active. The frontal lobes, the part of our brain associated with complex thinking actually registers a drop in activity.

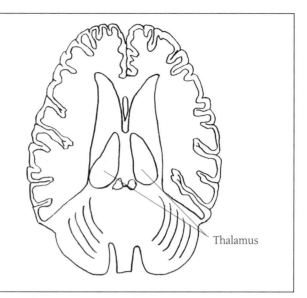

Thalamus

turn on the light for a moment to calm down. Now go back into the battle. Do not concede. Return to the pillow and consciously return to the events of the dream only this time, sword in hand, make sure you prevail. Remember, you have control, not the monsters. Slay them.

If you stick with it, and fight your fear, this procedure will work and although you may occasionally still have a bad dream, you will never again be dominated.

You will know what to do and how to do it. You will simply redirect the dream just like a Hollywood Mogul overriding an upstart director. You'll make sure there's a bona fide, crowd-pleasing happy ending. (None of that film noir stuff as long as you're running the studio!)

I can't promise you'll ever resolve your maternal conflicts, but at least you'll get a good night's sleep, even when she's visiting.

The Meaning of a Dream

2

Upon waking, the vast majority of our dreams are already forgotten, gone from our consciousness like the insignificant events of the past day.

A very few stick with us after we open our eyes. But most of those are also gone from our short-term memory within twenty minutes.

Still, every so often, a dream stays with us for a while longer. If we ponder over it enough, we might remember it for the entire day or several days, even weeks or months if we find it particularly puzzling or disturbing.

In these cases, we have an uncomfortable suspicion that the dream has some kind of meaning for us. We may try to figure out what that meaning is or, if we are sufficiently unnerved, do our best to forget the dream altogether.

Some of us even go to elaborate lengths in hopes of discovering the meaning of our dream. We consult our friends, even consult so-called dream interpretation experts. The experience can become obsessive.

So do the dreams have meaning? If so, should our brains be concerned if they can't seem to understand the dream?

Some dreams definitely do appear to have a meaning.

One group of dream researchers believes that those dreams are actually messages being delivered from your silent right brain to your verbal left brain. This group includes many psychotherapists who would also tell you that you are likely suppressing some feelings.

What they are implying is that your logical left brain has been shutting out an input from your emotional right brain, at least during the day.

For some reason, during the sleep state, the right brain is able to override the left brain and get the message through.

This explanation is certainly plausible and would appear to hold true for some dreams.

Now, will figuring out this kind of dream help your brain? The answer is, maybe.

So go ahead and try to decode your dream if you want. But keep in mind the "meaning" of this kind of dream is very specific to your brain. Be very circumspect about seeking out other people's interpretation of your dream.

Despite the perceived difficulty, it is better that you trust your own brain and try to resolve the meaning for yourself. Only your brain can know for sure what message, if any, is present.

Here are some tips on how to proceed.

Think about the dream casually. Try not to attach great importance to the dream's resolution. Don't spend too much time thinking about it. Let your brain go on to other things. Get on with your daily life. Remember, the meaning of your dream is just as likely to come to you when you're not consciously thinking about it.

Next, remember that is just possible that the dream has no specific meaning or that you will not discover it. Let your brain know it's okay if it doesn't figure it out. Don't feel you have failed.

Besides, if the message is all that vitally important, it will likely be re-sent in a more intelligible form. You'll have another version of the dream and maybe then, with the new information, your brain will be able to figure it out.

Another thing that might help. Try doing some of the right–left brain exercises from Chapter 6 to help your brain open up a good clear communication channel.

It may even happen that the meaning of the dream will suddenly pop into your consciousness right in the middle of an exercise. It has happened for me, but I caution, that's only my personal experience.

Now for the other possibility. Not all dreams that we remember are messages in the sense that we just discussed.

Sometimes you remember a dream because the events were bizarre either in a silly or shocking way.

Perhaps a straight-laced friend of yours did a striptease or the day of the big party some disaster caused the event to be ruined.

Interpretation here is not the problem. It's more a matter that you feel a little embarrassed that your brain dared imagine such a thought, even if wasn't done consciously.

Chalk these dreams off to your brain letting off a little mischievous steam and just forget them. Unless of course you want to relate them to your friends for their amusement value.

Okay, now the last thing to consider is the famous pizza theory. That's the theory that overly spicy food may well have been the source for your amazingly vivid dream or dreams. How? I have no idea, but it certainly happens to me. These dreams mercifully fade fairly quickly, lasting about as long as the heartburn.

Finally, remember that we're not alone. Other animals also dream, including dogs and cats.

Whatever it's ultimate purpose, dreaming is obviously a basic brain function and apparently a necessary one.

So try not to fear your dreams or let them overwhelm you. Treat them as you would a sudden creative thought. Welcome them, enjoy them, learn from them, but recognize that they may not always pan out into something of value.

They're a renewable resource. Feel free to discard them.

Dreams of Success

Night dreaming can directly effect your waking performance both mentally and physically.

But did you know that you can take control of your night dreams in order to achieve a positive goal or banish a fear or even eliminate some unwanted behavior or habit?

Here's how you do it.

It's basically just a process of autosuggestion, not unlike self-hypnosis. What you want to do is plant positive thoughts in your brain before going to sleep so your brain can incorporate those thoughts during the night.

You start as you are undressing for bed. Banish the problems of the day and think only about the future and what it is you want to achieve. Think about a goal, a long-term goal or a short-term goal.

If it's long-term goal, you will be using this exercise as an extension of the day-dreaming exercise to "see" yourself in a new role, a successful role.

If it's a short-term goal, something that will be coming in the next few weeks, then you will be concentrating on a very specific action.

Let's say the goal is to do well on a test coming up next week. The first thing you need to be able to do is study productively. So you go to bed imagining yourself waking up full of energy and enthusiasm for cracking the books. You envision yourself as being highly organized. You see yourself easily assimilating the information and even having extra time to relax after your work is done.

You then go to sleep imagining this very positive image of yourself. As you drift off, you see it happening. In fact, you can't wait to wake up and get to work.

The night before the actual exam, you concentrate your thoughts on acing it. You know your mind will be in top form, ready to go. You see yourself working intensely, steadily, confidently. Plant those thoughts in your mind and dream sweet dreams of success.

Remember, more than half the battle is confidence. And not only is this is a very good way to build up your brain's confidence, but it also lets your brain get a good night's sleep which means you'll be fresh and ready to go.

Variations on this procedure work for changing habits such as smoking or overcoming fears, such as fear of flying. Create positive images and your brain will absorb those images while you sleep.

A note on the specific technique for eliminating an unwanted fear.

Banishing a fear is more often than not a gradual process because the circuits that trigger fear are so strongly laid down in the brain. Permanently overriding them takes time.

And during the early attempts to use dreaming as a redirection method, there is always the risk of triggering a nightmare.

But take heart, this actually gives you a strong opportunity to make some quick progress.

Follow the instructions in the section on "controlling unruly dreams" to turn the nightmare into a positive scenario of you overcoming the fearful event.

If you dream about a plane crashing, get back in that plane and make it land safely. You can do it.

Just remember, if you show courage in your dream, that courage will carry over. You will awake stronger and more confident than ever before.

Remember your brain keeps on working while you're asleep. You might as well put it to some good use.

4 *Self-Hypnosis*

The question is why would you pay someone to hypnotize your brain when you can do the same thing yourself? Many people do and swear by the results.

Don't worry, you won't start clucking like a chicken, that is unless you tell yourself to. Remember, you are going to be planting as well as receiving the suggestions. Seem a little weird, maybe even scary?

Relax, a hypnotic or trance state is not all that mysterious or even unusual. In fact, many religions urge their followers to practice self-hypnosis, believing it to be a way of opening a window to the soul, and to the eternal.

Whether or not that's true, a trance state does put the brain into a highly concentrated state where thoughts seem to penetrate to the deeper levels almost instantaneously.

That means that a simple suggestion, for example "I am a non-smoker," can immediately become something that seems a part of us, something we always knew or believed or did.

Conversely, we can also pull information out of the deepest part of our memory system while in this hypnotic state. We can sometimes retrieve elusive memories, even suddenly recall the location of an important object that we have mislaid.

That's the power of this strange and exotic mental state. So if you want to try it out, but are short of funds or just shy and prefer to attempt it solo in the privacy of your own home, here's the drill. Oh, and by the way, it doesn't hurt or even feel weird. In fact, it's actually very pleasant and restful, like taking a nap.

You hypnotize yourself pretty much the same way a practitioner would do it.

You find a quiet comfortable spot, sit or lie down and stare at a gently swinging object like a metronome. You can also use a softly blinking light. Hey! Finally a use for that annoying clock on the VCR! You know the one you can't figure out how to stop from flashing 12:00 all the time. It's just the ticket for self-hypnosis. And if some annoying friend or relative has inconveniently set it for you, no problem. Just pull the plug out of the wall and then put it back in. Voila! Instant power failure!

Okay, now concentrate your mind on the swinging or flashing object. Tell yourself to relax. Tell yourself you are sleepy. Yes, just like in the movies.

If you concentrate hard and keep doing this you will find your mind suddenly pops into a, well, a trance.

You will be fully aware but your mind will be marvelously concentrated. Now you can if you want do nothing and just enjoy it. It is extremely restful and refreshing, just like taking a nap.

Or you could take the opportunity to stick in some useful suggestions, like "you will like doing the laundry." Up to you.

"Nothing contributes so much to tranquilize the mind as a steady purpose—a point on which the soul may fix its intellectual eye."
—Mary Wollenstonecraft Shelley

When you want to come out of it, you just wake up. The thought that you want to stop is enough. You see you have actually been doing something very like sleeping only less so, or more so? You tell me.

Happy trance.

Oh, and if you have trouble, you may need less distraction. Try a darkened room that is reasonably soundproof. You'll eventually get there. We all have the ability. It's just easier for some of us than others.

CHAPTER 16

Brain Rest and a Final Word About Introspection

How To Shut It Down and Take a Break

Resting the brain after intensive use is as important as resting you muscles after a workout.

Sometimes the rest called for is the same as it is for the physical body, some good sound sleep. Other times a relaxing bath is as soothing to the brain as it is to the body.

"It is sweet to let the mind unbend on occasion."

—Horace

But other times your mind is racing from it's recent activity and you just can't shut it down. It just wants to go on and on even though it's so wound up that it's just spinning it's wheels. You know it's time to rest but you can't find a way to shut it down. It's times like this that you wish there was a master switch. If you're desperate enough, you might be tempted to use a chemical extinguisher; a drug will sometimes do the trick but it's a dangerous choice.

Now I'm not saying that a judicious drink or two of alcohol is necessarily bad. Medically, a couple of drinks, if you can keep it to that, is actually good for your body and your brain.

But if you're really frazzled, the temptation is to drink yourself into a stupor and that is not good. So let's examine some alternatives. Some ways to fight fire with fire. Use the

207

brain to calm itself down. Ways to get it to shift itself into a soothing, restful state.

There are also some things that the body can do to help, or rather there are some things you can do to your body that will help relax your brain.

Below are some suggestions. Pick out what works for your brain.

The Exercises

EXERCISE

1

Opposing Action

Often when we experience mental fatigue it's just because we have been overusing one particular mental facility. We all know we can get eye strain from too much reading, especially in poor light. But we can also fatigue the brain from an activity like reading.

If we are reading highly sequential or logical information with few or no diagrams or pictures to break it up, then we are relying heavily on our left-brain functions with hardly any help at all from our right brain. This naturally fatigues the left brain. But rest or sleep is not necessarily the antidote. The right brain is still fresh as a daisy and may even resist the idea. The problem here is one of balance. You need to reverse the flow, turn off as much of the left-brain circuits as you can and crank up the right brain.

So how do you do that? You put down the book, get up, and look for some large scale visual stimulation. You take a walk outside if possible where there are trees and scenery. You avoid people and conversation because that will engage too much of your left brain. You simply stroll, making your mind a blank except that your eyes are open wide, taking in the view. You breathe deeply, taking in the smells and you listen to the sounds of nature. Twenty minutes later, you feel like you had a good night's sleep. Why? Because the balance was restored. If it's the dead of winter and you can't go out, another way to do it is with soothing music that kicks in good strong right-brain feelings. For some people, looking at pictures or even reading poetry can do the exact same thing.

Now exactly the opposite can be true. Intense right-brain activity such as pattern-matching, map-reading, engaging in large visual and spatial projects, master planning where you are trying to grasp the whole cause your right brain to become fatigued.

Another killer is intensive social interaction where you are constantly required to read people's moods. Like at work when you are thinking. "Is the boss receptive right now? Is it a good time to unveil my new plan or should I wait till later?"

All this kind of activity is very wearing on the right brain. The result is that you crave some quiet time alone with something logical and sequential. For some that's a good nonfiction book or newspaper article. For others it's a pleasing routine like making dinner. It could be a crossword puzzle or playing on the computer. Maybe sitting down and going over the finances or planning the details of an upcoming vacation. You get the idea. Figure out what you were doing, what brain circuits it involved, and try to engage the opposite side.

The good news is that even if you can't figure it out, your brain can. It will tell you what it needs. It will simply want to do something. Just follow your instinct and let it do what it needs to do even if that means staring blankly at the wall for ten minutes. If it's what the brain needs, it will be refreshing and you will come back stronger and ready for more work.

If it's the end of your work period and the problem is your brain just won't shut down, what you need is a diversion.

If you have some friends that you know are always up for a good time, call them and arrange to meet. If that isn't possible, try turning on the television. Look for something easy to watch that holds your attention and gets your brain off of thoughts of work.

If that doesn't do it, then take a walk in a busy area with lots of people around. Go to a shopping street or a mall and browse. Go into stores with lots of colorful merchandise that holds some interest for you. If you want, pretend you are shopping for a new wardrobe and try a bunch of clothes on, but take my advice on this one, leave the credit cards at home.

EXERCISE

2

Using the Physical to Shut Down the Mental

Another opposite is the physical. Intensive mental tasks involving very little muscle activity quite naturally make the body and the brain crave physical movement.

Many people find the best antidote for a hard day's brain-work is a good physical workout. The obvious added benefit is that it's very good for your health.

Now a physical workout can be anything from a brisk walk to a jog, to a trip to the gym, to a game of basketball or tennis. Whatever it is that you enjoy and your body will allow, try to make a habit of it. That way, just the suggestion that you are going out for a bike ride will be enough to calm your brain.

Now, for those times that you're stuck in the office and can't stray that far, sometimes just stretching and deep breathing can offer mental and physical relief. In fact, taking a regular stretch break can make a major difference in your general productivity. Here's a couple of easy tips.

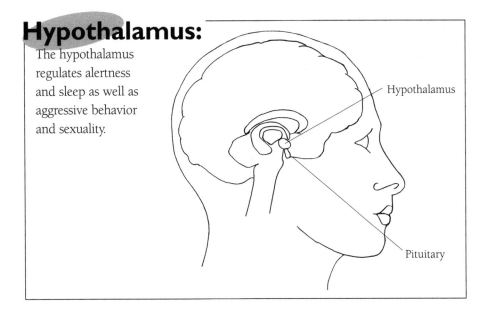

Hypothalamus:

The hypothalamus regulates alertness and sleep as well as aggressive behavior and sexuality.

Hypothalamus

Pituitary

If you can, lay down on the floor on your back. Pull your knees up to your chest one at a time and hold for thirty seconds. This will take the tension out of your lower back. Next roll over and sit up on your knees. Put your arms out in front of you, and your head down. Reach out and put your hands flat on the floor as far away as you can, rocking up on your knees as you go. Now pull your head and shoulders down toward the ground. This will stretch out your shoulders and upper arms. Now stand up and run in place vigorously for a few minutes.

If your room has a door, go over and reach up and grab the upper frame, get hold of the molding if you can. Pull down on it. Test it. If it's strong enough to take your weight, go ahead and hang for a moment. If not, just sag your body and let your arms stretch as much as possible without breaking the door frame.

Take a couple of deep breaths and you're done.

3

Meditation, A Mental Rubdown

Another way to relax the neural circuits and put the brain into a low-energy state is the process known as meditation.

Meditation has many guises and many purposes, some of them spiritual and some of them designed to imprint positive thoughts upon the brain.

So what is meditation?

It's basically a more focused version of daydreaming, but not quite so focused as the full trance state induced by hypnosis (although it can come close, depending on the practitioner's desire and skill.)

But we are not concerned here with so lofty a goal as either spiritual awareness or empowering our minds to succeed.

Here we just want to discover how to use simple meditation to relax the brain and let it get some needed rest. Fortunately, to do that is fairly easy.

Here's how to do it.

The simplest technique is to sit back comfortably, close your eyes, and envision a peaceful scene, either from memory or from imagination.

Example: You are in the midst of a nasty winter. It's cold out, it's dark out, and you are stuck facing a hard evening of overtime at the office. You need something to pep you up and get you through. Your brain is fried.

Okay, you stop for a moment, close your eyes, and imagine a beautiful warm beach with a glorious warm sun shining down. You meditate on it, that is you let your mind revel in the imagined feeling for, say, five solid minutes.

Then you slowly release the image and reopen your eyes.

Suddenly your mind feels rested. Your mood has brightened. Your spirits are lifted. Why, you're feeling downright perky. You still have to face the work, but now you have fresh energy and a smile on your face. That beach was good.

In a similar manner or at a different time, you might prefer the image of plunging into a cool pool of clear water or laying in the snow with the cool, cold air invigorating your skin.

"The earth and myself are of one mind."
—Chief Joseph

If you are a homebody, you might want to imagine lying comfortably in a soothing bath with your favorite music playing.

You can use any image at all, so long as it is pleasing to you and restful to your mind. The idea is to capture the complete picture in your mind and then dwell on it. But remember to make it restful. Do not turn it into an action scene where you are doing things. That requires too much brain use.

Think more of how it would feel to be in the scene and resting. The way you might really lie on a beach on a real vacation. Restful, peaceful, napping. No gorgeous bodies allowed, no fast cars, no winning lottery tickets. The idea here is the mind at rest.

Now this form of meditation is easy to practice and fairly effective. However, there are a few other methods that some people feel are even more effective. But I warn you, they require a little more effort, a little more practice, a little more skill.

For example, in one version you attempt to completely empty your mind of all thought. You try to merge your mind with nothingness, literally become nonexistent. This is a form of Zen and you can easily find knowledgeable practitioners just dying to give you further instruction. But you can also just try it and see how you do.

Another way of meditating is to center on a particular thought, a few words, a line of poetry, something that strikes your mind as timeless and profound.

You simply let the thought and the feeling it invokes fill your entire mind like a growing light. Now obviously the thought should be a positive profundity. Subjects like death and the emptiness of the universe may well launch you into a spiritual state, but I can't recommend them for relaxation.

The final one I am going to mention here is the famous meaningless word, or mantra.

This comes to us from Buddhism. Now if you're a real Buddhist, someone in authority is suppose to chose your mantra for you and give it to you. They then tell you to keep it a deep secret. It's yours and yours alone.

What they don't tell you is that there are a finite number of mantras which means, of course, that thousands of people are trespassing daily on your private meditation channel. But it's okay because you don't know that. Whoops, I guess I told you.

Okay, so assuming you are not looking for enlightenment but just want to rest some very tired neurons, pick a meaningless word, repeat it over and over to yourself and focus your mind on the sound. Personally, I prefer the beach, but to each his own.

Taking Direct Action

4

A full-body massage or even just a simple backrub can be surprisingly invigorating and renewing for the brain.

Sometimes when your brain is really stressed, the feeling of giving your body over to a pair of comfortable, experienced hands can be just what the doctor ordered.

And if you find your budget doesn't allow for a professional job and your better half is suffering from carpal tunnel syndrome, then there is nothing to do but take the matter in your own hands and give yourself a direct brain massage.

Oh yes, you can do it and it feels terrific. I do it myself twice a day and if I could only find a way to bottle and sell it, I would probably become a rich man.

But as you were kind enough to buy this book, I'm going to let you in on my secret technique at no additional charge. Here's what you do.

Sitting or standing doesn't matter. Take your two hands, lift them in the air, and place just your fingertips firmly on your scalp, slightly toward the back. Place one hand on the right side, one on the left. Both brain halves get equal treatment.

Now still just using just your fingertips tighten your grip. (I know, it feels very strange to grab hold of your skull and squeeze, but trust me, it will pay off.)

Okay, shake your hands and vibrate your fingers vigorously while holding on to your scalp for dear life. (Please note, vibrate and shake only, no violent jerking or whipping. I don't want any sprained necks.)

Don't let go and don't fight your hands. Just give in to the motion. Now close your eyes and bow your head forward. Relax your thoughts. Pretend another person is massaging your head.

Keep up the motion for at least two minutes at which point your hand muscles are probably getting very tired.

Ease off and let your hands come down to your side. Keep your eyes closed and your head bowed while you count to twenty. Raise your head while taking in a deep breath. Now slowly exhale. That's it, you're done. You just gave yourself a brain massage!

Now with practice you might be able to build up strength and get your hands to keep up the shaking action a little longer. (That's between you, your brain, and your hands.)

You will also please note that your hair was not mussed during this vigorous exercise, that is, if you were doing it right. (Fingers tight to the scalp at all times.)

That was no accident. I purposely designed this exercise to be coiffeur-friendly because the last thing our brains need is for the boss to walk in and see us looking like we just had a quick roll in the hay.

So there you have it. Your brain gets a good rubdown and your hair stays neat! What more could you ask for?

EXERCISE

5

A Final Word on Introspection

One major brain function that we haven't talked about so far in this exercise book is the process known as introspection.

Sooner or later we all come to it. We take stock. We look at who we are, and where we have come from. We think about what we have done or not done and we think about where we are going from here.

We think about what is yet to be done and what it is we want to accomplish with our future.

"By a tranquil mind I mean nothing else than a mind well-ordered."—Marcus Aurelius

It's a natural brain function, introspection, something that we do from time to time and something that serves a very positive purpose. It helps us to see ourselves larger, to see the grand and wondrous journey we are on.

But there is a danger to be mentioned here. Not with introspection, but with it's nemesis, rumination.

Rumination seems very like introspection except that the thoughts are all turned around. When we ruminate, we think about what we didn't do, what we failed to do, and what we can't do. We dwell on our shortcomings and our bad luck. We see the world as hostile and ourselves as helpless victims. We ruminate on our hapless and sorry fate.

Rumination is a negative mind state and no good can ever come from it. It is to be avoided like the plague.

It serves no practical purpose and does neither the mind nor the body any good whatsoever.

In fact, it does the mind great harm. It undermines confidence and breeds an attitude of defeatism.

It pits our mind against itself. We become split off from ourselves. We stand apart and criticize who we are and what we are.

This is one brain process you must guard against. Simply don't allow it.

And if you find your brain lapsing into rumination, stop it immediately. Don't let the process continue.

Turn those negative thoughts to positive ones. Be constructive. If you have had failures, then take lessons from them and move on. The past is done, leave it behind. Do not dwell on things you cannot do or have not the power to change. Instead, turn your mind to the future and to what you can do and will do.

Treat that brain of yours with the respect it deserves and it will serve you better than you can ever imagine. Remember, your brain is potentially as good as any brain on the planet. So be proud of it. And keep it in good working order. Keep it well-exercised.

May your neurons be many and well connected,

Snowdon Parlette